COME OUT FROM AMONG THEM

Book 1

THE DANGERS OF NOT PRACTICING CHURCH DISCIPLINE

Charles Morris

Copyright © 2024 Charles W Morris

All rights reserved. No part of this book may be used or reproduced by any means, graphic, electronic, or mechanical, including photocopying, recording, taping, or by any information storage retrieval system without the written permission of the publisher except in the case of brief quotations embodied in critical articles and reviews.

Scriptures are taken from the English Standard Version of the Bible

Books may be ordered through booksellers or by contacting:
RSIP
Raising the Standard International Publishing L. L. C.
https://www.rsipublishing.com

RSIP-Charles Morris
https://www.rsiministry.com
Navarre, Florida

ISBN: 9781960641557
Printed in the United States of America
Edition Date: August 2024

Contents

1	The Command To "Be Ye Holy"	1
2	Who Are Our Friends & Who Are Our Enemies?	7
3	Choose Either God or "Not God"	19
4	Avoid Unruly Christians; Romans 16:17-18	33
5	Keep Away From Unruly Christians; 2 Thessalonians 3:6 Part 1	38
6	Keep Away From Unruly Christians; 2 Thessalonians 3:6 Part 2	43
7	Have Nothing To Do With Unruly Christians; 2 Thessalonians 3:14-15 & Titus 3:10-11	48
8	Do Not Associate With Unruly Christians; 1 Corinthians 5:9-13 Part 1	50
9	Do Not Associate With Unruly Christians; 1 Corinthians 5:9-13 Part 2	52
10	Do Not Associate With Unruly Christians; 1 Corinthians 5:9-13 Part 3	56
11	Do Not Associate With Unruly Christians; 1 Corinthians 5:9-13 Part 4	61
12	Do Not Associate With Unruly Christians; 1 Corinthians 5:9-13 Part 5	64
13	Do Not Associate With Unruly Christians; 1 Corinthians 5:9-13 Part 6	70
14	Do Not Associate With Unruly Christians; 1 Corinthians 5:9-13 Part 7	78
15	Do Not Associate With Unruly Christians; 1 Corinthians 5:9-13 Part 8	81

16	Do Not Associate With Unruly Christians; 1 Corinthians 5:9-13 Part 9	86
17	Withdraw From Those That Teach Unsound Doctrine; 1 Timothy 6:3-5 Part 1	91
18	Withdraw From Those That Teach Unsound Doctrine; 1 Timothy 6:3-5 Part 2	94
19	Withdraw From Those That Teach Unsound Doctrine; 1 Timothy 6:3-5 Part 3	100
20	Withdraw From Those That Teach Unsound Doctrine; 1 Timothy 6:3-5 Part 4	103
21	Withdraw From Those That Teach Unsound Doctrine; 1 Timothy 6:3-5 Part 5	106
22	Withdraw From Those That Teach Unsound Doctrine; 1 Timothy 6:3-5 Part 6	110
23	Withdraw From Those That Teach Unsound Doctrine; 1 Timothy 6:3-5 Part 7	114
	More Books By Charles Morris	119
	About The Author	123

Chapter 1

The Command To "Be Ye Holy"

We are to "Come out from among them." Do what? Precisely what does this mean? Charles, this title sounds divisive and judgmental. Okay, now that I have gotten your attention, let me say that this might be one of the most difficult and challenging books you have ever read.

I want to preface this book with these statements, which must be remembered throughout this reading. This book should not be used as a witch hunt or vindictive source against those who violate our pet peeve sins. The material in this book is not to promote or validate self-righteousness in those who feel they are above the sinful practices listed. This book's material is not to justify someone seeking to dismiss pastoral leadership, cause division within the fellowship, or split a church. The material contained in this book is a clear Biblical directive for Christians to act like Christians, and those who do not are subject to church discipline, according to Matthew 18:15-20. In all matters of the Christian faith, we are commanded to do so in love and not vindictiveness. The end result of church discipline should always be about redemption and reconciliation.

Do I believe the Bible teaches love and unity? Yes! Do I believe God's Word teaches us that we should seek to be at peace with all men? Again, yes. Do I believe God's Word will unite all who embrace and walk in it? Absolutely yes.

However, I also believe the Bible teaches church discipline and warnings for believers who refuse to embrace the mandate of "be holy as I am holy."

In a day when "we need unity," are you asking me to break fellowship with my friends? But wait a minute. Didn't Jesus tell us that our greatest enemies would be members of our households and that He did not come to bring peace but a sword that would divide? I could go on and on with questions and comments on the subject of "Come out from among them."

> Matthew 10:34-36 (ESV) "Do not think that I have come to bring peace to the earth. I have not come to bring peace, but a sword. 35 For I have come to set a man against his father, and a daughter against her mother, and a daughter-in-law against her mother-in-law. 36 And a person's enemies will be those of his own household.

The concept of unity in our modern-day teachings has been misconstrued, advocating for a constant association with anyone at all times. However, the guidance from the Word of God directs us to discern and separate ourselves from certain individuals. Come out from among them! This is a blast against our emotional and theological belief that God wants unity at all costs.

This study aims to identify those individuals from whom we are called to distance ourselves in order to fulfill the divine purpose set forth by our heavenly Father. This is Book 1 of a two-book series titled *"Come Out From Among Them."* As God's Word describes, the embodiment of a fruitful, holy, and blessed Christian is contingent upon leading a sanctified (set apart), holy, and undefiled daily walk with our Lord.

The commentary approach provided is intentional, as the objective is to allow the Scriptures themselves to convey the message. The passages presented are not a product of personal opinion but are delivered from the Word of God, intended for our spiritual growth and protection against defilement caused by sensual pleasures, unfruitful traditions, and the doctrines of men and demons. A reflection on the seven churches in Revelation chapters 2 and 3 underscores the consequences of embracing such teachings, leading to a rebuke from our Lord.

While portraying ourselves as spiritual by waiting for a "Word from the Lord" or "being led by the Holy Spirit" before distancing ourselves from a place or individual, this study emphasizes that we already possess the mandate in the Scriptures to obey. The proclamation of waiting for divine guidance is in opposition to the reality that the Father awaits our obedience to what He has already communicated.

Referencing King David's insights in Psalm 1, the study highlights God's plan for the Christian walk. As people of faith, our companions should be those who carry faith in their hearts. The term "Blessed" conveys a sense of happiness and fortune in the Lord. Psalm 1 portrays three distinct positions we are commanded not to engage in – walking with, standing with, or sitting with certain groups. This scriptural guidance forms the basis for understanding the boundaries and associations that align with God's divine plan for believers.

> *Psalms 1:1-3 (ESV) Blessed is the man who **walks not** in the counsel of the wicked, **nor stands** in the way of sinners, **nor sits** in the seat of scoffers; 2 but his delight is in the law of the LORD, and on his law he meditates day and night. 3 He is like a tree planted by streams of water that yields its fruit in its season, and its leaf does not wither. In all that he does, he prospers.*

> *Psalms 1:4-6 (ESV) The wicked are not so, but are like chaff that the wind drives away. 5 Therefore the wicked will not stand in the judgment, nor sinners in the congregation of the righteous; 6 for the LORD knows the way of the righteous, but the way of the wicked will perish.*

Notice that Psalm 1 does not tell us to be unloving towards the three groups listed. It is not a matter of loving them. We are to love our Christian brothers and sisters, and we are to love our enemies. Somewhere in our Christian theology, we have adopted the idea that because we are commanded to love someone, then we are commanded to fellowship and walk with them. As we will see from God's Word, nothing could be farther from the truth.

The Book of Proverbs provides numerous warnings about the allure of temptation and emphasizes our role in choosing the path we follow. Each moment of our daily lives presents a choice between succumbing to the deeds of the flesh or aligning ourselves by walking in the Spirit and manifesting the fruit of the Holy Spirit.

> *Proverbs 1:10-15 (ESV) My son, if sinners entice you, **do not consent**. 11 If they say, "Come with us, let us lie in wait for blood; let us ambush the innocent*

> *without reason; 12 like Sheol let us swallow them alive, and whole, like those who go down to the pit; 13 we shall find all precious goods, we shall fill our houses with plunder; 14 throw in your lot among us; we will all have one purse"— 15 my son,* **do not walk in the way with them; hold back your foot from their paths**,

Proverbs 4 employs terms such as "avoid it," "pass not by it," "turn from it," and "pass away" to articulate the actions we should take in response to sin and association with sinful individuals. This is also seen in Proverbs 13, where walking with the wise is contrasted with walking with fools and sinners.

> *Proverbs 4:13-16 (ESV) Keep hold of instruction; do not let go; guard her, for she is your life. 14* **Do not enter the path of the wicked, and do not walk in the way of the evil**. *15* **Avoid it; do not go on it; turn away from it and pass on**. *16 For they cannot sleep unless they have done wrong; they are robbed of sleep unless they have made someone stumble.*

> *Proverbs 13:20-22 (ESV)* **Whoever walks with the wise becomes wise**, *but* **the companion of fools will suffer harm**. *21* **Disaster pursues sinners**, *but the righteous are rewarded with good. 22 A good man leaves an inheritance to his children's children, but the sinner's wealth is laid up for the righteous.*

The urgency of these instructions echoes a resonant cry akin to the prophet Isaiah's impassioned plea in Isaiah 52 to the nation of God's people. Isaiah fervently implores, "Depart ye, depart ye, go ye out from thence, touch no unclean thing; go ye out of the midst of her; be ye clean, that bear the vessels of the LORD." This powerful call to separation and cleanliness is a vivid reminder of the imperative to distance ourselves from sin and maintain a purity that befits those who bear the vessels of the Lord. The intricate interplay of wisdom literature and prophetic exhortation underscores the timeless significance of choosing a righteous path and heeding the call to depart from the ways of sin.

> *Isaiah 52:10-12 (ESV) The LORD has bared his holy arm before the eyes of all the nations, and all the ends of the earth shall see the salvation of our God. 11* **<u>Depart, depart, go out from there; touch no unclean thing; go out from the midst of her; purify yourselves, you who bear the vessels of the LORD</u>**<u>.</u> *12 For you shall not go out in haste, and you shall not go in flight, for the LORD will go before you, and the God of Israel will be your rear guard.*

The bottom line is this.

Come Out From Among Them

Chapter 2

Who Are Our Friends & Who Are Our Enemies?

We are instructed to extend love not only to our friends but also to our adversaries. Although commanded to love them, it is Biblically taboo to fellowship with our enemies. True Biblical fellowship with the Lord and fellow believers emerges when we are recognized as friends of God. It is crucial to acknowledge that there are individuals who stand as enemies to God, consequently becoming our enemies by default. Despite this, we are commanded to exhibit love and offer prayers for those the Bible calls our adversaries.

> *Matthew 5:43-47 (ESV) "You have heard that it was said, 'You shall love your neighbor and hate your enemy.' 44 But I say to you, **Love your enemies and pray for those who persecute you,** 45 so that you may be sons of your Father who is in heaven. For he makes his sun rise on the evil and on the good, and sends rain on the just and on the unjust. 46 For if you love those who love you, what reward do you have? Do not even the tax collectors do the same? 47 And if you greet only your brothers, what more are you doing than others? Do not even the Gentiles do the same?*

NOTE! It's important to note that in a Biblical context, enemies are not confined to those who may have caused us harm. Often, we narrow down our list of enemies to those who have inflicted emotional, mental, relational, physical, financial, or spiritual harm upon us. However, this doesn't align with the Biblical understanding of enemies. While there may be those who harbor hatred and mistreat us, they do not constitute the entirety of what the Bible refers to as enemies.

> *Luke 6:22-23 (ESV) "Blessed are you when people hate you and when they exclude you and revile you and spurn your name as evil, on account of the Son of Man! 23 Rejoice in that day, and leap for joy, for behold, your reward is great in heaven; for so their fathers did to the prophets.*

According to the Scriptures, all spiritually lost individuals are deemed enemies to God, and consequently, they should be considered as our enemies. Similarly, believers who immerse themselves in worldly pursuits and values are also regarded as enemies of God. It might be challenging to accept this perspective at first, but it is essential to delve into the teachings of God's Word. If there are reservations about this concept, it is encouraged to seek guidance from the Father, who authored the guidelines.

Our Enemies

The issue at hand revolves around this challenge. Within the community of believers, some individuals who are expected to be our friends exhibit behaviors, speech, and attitudes akin to enemies, eroding the trust that should naturally exist. There are supposed friends among believers whose actions and words deviate from the expected norm of someone walking with God, creating an atmosphere of mistrust. Though these individuals profess to be on the same spiritual journey, they display traits and behaviors inconsistent with genuine friendship, leading to doubts about their reliability and sincerity as Christian brothers and sisters in the Lord.

On the other hand, some adversaries disguise themselves as allies, adopting a façade of friendship while concealing their true intentions. In other words, they are *"wolves in sheep's clothing."* One of the terms you will read many times in this book is "The fruit reveals the root."

> Matthew 7:15-18 (ESV) *"Beware of false prophets,* **who come to you in sheep's clothing but inwardly are ravenous wolves.** *16 You will recognize them by their fruits. Are grapes gathered from thornbushes, or figs from thistles? 17 So, every healthy tree bears good fruit, but the diseased tree bears bad fruit. 18 A healthy tree cannot bear bad fruit, nor can a diseased tree bear good fruit.*

Beware Of The Pretenders

It may be difficult for some of us to believe some folks pose as friends within the Christian community but harbor ulterior motives. These individuals intentionally adopt a deceptive guise, portraying themselves as allies while concealing their true identities as adversaries. Their actions mimic those of genuine friends, making it challenging to discern their true intentions and posing a potential threat to the trust and cohesion within the community of believers.

Navigating this complex dynamic requires a discerning spirit and a careful evaluation of actions and words. We are to be "fruit inspectors." It prompts believers to be vigilant in distinguishing genuine friendship from deceptive pretenses.

It is imperative that we exercise caution in placing our trust in certain individuals. However, the key lies in seeking discernment from the Father to identify them accurately. A crucial question arises in this quest for clarity: "Are you a friend or an enemy?" Delving into the teachings of the Word becomes essential in answering this query.

Do Not Love The World Or The Things Of The World

The Scriptures unequivocally state that those who align themselves as friends of the world are, in turn, deemed enemies of God. This correlation implies that if someone stands as an adversary to God, they consequently become enemies to us as well. Therefore, the alignment of an individual with the values and pursuits of the world prompts a recognition of their status as enemies to God and ourselves. It should be noted that James was speaking to Christian brothers and sisters within the fellowship.

> *James 4:4 (ESV) You adulterous people! Do you not know that **friendship with the world is enmity with God**? Therefore **whoever wishes to be a friend of the world makes himself an enemy of God**.*

In navigating these considerations, the call is for a deeper understanding of the Word to discern the true nature of individuals and the values they espouse. By grounding our judgments on the teachings of the Scriptures, we can gain clarity in distinguishing between friends and potential adversaries. Being a people of the Word and the Spirit assists in ultimately aligning ourselves with those who share a genuine commitment to the divine principles outlined in God's Word.

The Scriptures further expound that individuals who harbor a love for the world or are entangled in worldly pursuits do not genuinely love God, regardless of how frequently they verbalize such sentiments. The profound teachings underscore that mere lip service professing love for God falls short when contradicted by an affection for the values and attractions of the world.

> 1 John 2:15-17 (ESV) **Do not love the world or the things in the world. If anyone loves the world, the love of the Father is not in him**. 16 For all that is in the world—the desires of the flesh and the desires of the eyes and pride of life—is not from the Father but is from the world. 17 And the world is passing away along with its desires, but whoever does the will of God abides forever.

> Matthew 15:7-9 (ESV) You hypocrites! Well did Isaiah prophesy of you, when he said: 8 "'**This people honors me with their lips, but their heart is far from me**; 9 in vain do they worship me, teaching as doctrines the commandments of men.'"

Having spiritual insight prompts an examination of one's actions and affections, urging believers to go beyond surface declarations of love for God. The Scriptures emphasize that authentic love for our heavenly Father cannot coexist with a deep-seated attachment to worldly pleasures or ideologies. The discrepancy between verbal professions and observable conduct necessitates sincere self-examination. This self-examination should compel individuals to align their hearts and actions with a genuine devotion to God, which goes beyond superficial expressions of faith.

Despite the verbal assertions of some Christians professing love for God, a profound disconnection exists between the sentiments expressed on their lips and the actual state of their hearts. Religious activity is null and void if their hearts remain distant from fellowshipping with the Father. This prompts us to exercise personal responsibility in dealing with individuals who may be considered enemies.

Navigating The Biblical Mandates Concerning Fellowship & Friendship

In accordance with Biblical teachings, the mandate is clear. We are certainly to extend love even to those called by God to be our enemies. However, it is crucial to discern that this obligation to love does not necessarily translate into an obligation to engage in frequent social interactions or fellowship with them. The understanding is that while loving them is a Biblical mandate, the dynamics of the association are prescribed from God's Word so that there is no fellowship with them.

Therefore, believers find themselves navigating a delicate balance. We are to love our enemies as instructed, yet exercising discernment in determining the extent of social involvement is needed. Of course, we are commanded to interact with the spiritually lost. When it comes to our adversaries, the primary objective is to consistently present Jesus Christ and convey the profound message of the gospel. We must communicate the necessity of repentance from sins without engaging in sin. Remember that the definition of sin is a transgression against the commands of our Heavenly Father, both in His Word and His character. The central emphasis must remain on us actively sharing the redemptive message of our Lord Jesus Christ with those we perceive as enemies of God. This endeavor should be driven by the desire to see their lives changed with the spiritual significance found in Christ and being born again.

This calls for a thoughtful approach that upholds the principle of love without compromising personal boundaries or exposing oneself to potential emotional, mental, or spiritual harm. The gospel message is one of love tempered with wisdom, acknowledging the command to love enemies while maintaining a Biblical and discerning perspective on the nature and extent of personal engagement. In this, we answer the "why" question for seeking fellowship with the world and those who are spiritually lost.

The following statement is sad but true. It is disheartening to note that the Scriptures caution us about a sobering reality – that among our most formidable opponents may be individuals within our households. This reality underscores the importance of maintaining a steadfast commitment to sharing the gospel, even in the face of challenges that may emerge within the closest circles of our lives. The call is to persevere in the mission of presenting Christ, recognizing that this mission extends to all, even those who may, regrettably, be counted among our own household as adversaries.

> *Matthew 10:34-39 (ESV) "Do not think that I have come to bring peace to the earth. **I have not come to bring peace, but a sword.** 35 For I have come to set*

*a man against his father, and a daughter against her mother, and a daughter-in-law against her mother-in-law. 36 And **a person's enemies will be those of his own household.** 37 Whoever loves father or mother more than me is not worthy of me, and whoever loves son or daughter more than me is not worthy of me. 38 And whoever does not take his cross and follow me is not worthy of me. 39 Whoever finds his life will lose it, and whoever loses his life for my sake will find it.*

Profession Does Not Necessarily Mean Possession

If we merely profess knowledge of Christ as our Savior, it does not necessarily equate to truly possessing Him as one's Savior. The Bible lays out a vital distinction – prayer alone does not bring about salvation; it is through Jesus that salvation is realized. Prayers don't save us. Faith in the finished work of Christ saves us. Additionally, a paradox exists where some individuals, though saved, fall short in embodying the transformative power of their newfound life. To put it in simple terms, they called on the name of Jesus to be saved but have now grown past being an infant.

A common occurrence is the discrepancy between the profession of being a Christian, denoting Christlikeness, and the tangible expression of that belief in daily living. Many claim to be followers of Christ, acknowledging faith in God and the Bible, yet their actions and lifestyle betray a misalignment with these professed beliefs. This contradiction raises questions about the authenticity of their faith. In other words, if they were arrested for being a Christian, it is doubtful if there is enough evidence to convict them.

Come Out From Among Them

Matthew 7:21-23 (ESV) **"Not everyone who says to me, 'Lord, Lord,' will enter the kingdom of heaven,** *but the one who does the will of my Father who is in heaven. 22 On that day many will say to me, 'Lord, Lord, did we not prophesy in your name, and cast out demons in your name, and do many mighty works in your name?' 23 And* **then will I declare to them, 'I never knew you;** *depart from me, you workers of lawlessness.'*

While we might project an image of being God's friends to others, the reality may differ. True friendship with God extends beyond appearances. It encompasses an internal transformation aligned with His Word, influencing our inner life and external conduct. Again, I will say the fruit reveals the root. The reality lies in living according to the Father's precepts, allowing His Word to profoundly alter our thoughts, attitudes, and behaviors. The challenge is not merely to profess faith but to genuinely embody it, becoming living testimonies of the transformative power of God's Word in our lives.

The World Will Hate True Believers

Maintaining a genuine friendship with God involves more than merely acknowledging His existence; it necessitates an unwavering alignment with and obedience to His Word. Being God's friend is incompatible with dissent and rebellion against the divine teachings found in His Word. Hear what I just said. Disobeying the Father's commands using emotional justification does not align with a heart of love, obedience, and being called God's friend.

Furthermore, authentic friendship with God requires a departure from seeking approval and acceptance from the spiritually lost world. Seeking validation from those distant from God's truth is incongruent with a sincere commitment to divine principles. In essence, the desire for approval from the world contradicts the nature of being a friend of God.

Living in accordance with God's principles and faithfully practicing His Word inevitably draws the ire and persecution of the world. This is not an unexpected outcome; as Jesus forewarned, if the world harbored disdain for Him, those who genuinely follow Him should anticipate a similar response. The world, symbolized by those who are spiritually lost, will not readily embrace or approve of a life dedicated to God and His Word.

The unequivocal truth is that faithful followers of Jesus are destined to experience animosity from the world. This animosity is a testament to the stark contrast between living by divine principles versus conforming to the values of a spiritually lost world. In essence, embracing a genuine friendship with God entails embracing the likelihood of being unpopular or even despised by a world that stands at odds with the teachings of Christ.

> *2 Timothy 3:12-13 (ESV) Indeed, **all who desire to live a godly life in Christ Jesus will be persecuted**, 13 while evil people and impostors will go on from bad to worse, deceiving and being deceived.*

> *John 15:18-20 (ESV) "**If the world hates you, know that it has hated me before it hated you.** 19 If you were of the world, the world would love you as its own; but because you are not of the world, but I*

chose you out of the world, therefore **the world hates you.** *20 Remember the word that I said to you: 'A servant is not greater than his master.'* **If they persecuted me, they will also persecute you.** *If they kept my word, they will also keep yours.*

Suppose you find yourself untouched by criticism from those who are spiritually lost regarding your faith. In that case, it may indicate that you are not professing your faith in word and deed and not adhering to the principles outlined in the Word of God. Taking a stand on our beliefs becomes pivotal in the world. When we stand for nothing, we become susceptible to falling for anything.

Our assurance of persecution is grounded in the understanding that actively living out our faith and unwaveringly believing in the truths presented in God's Word will inevitably position us as adversaries to the world. Such a stance comes with the certainty that persecution will be part of our journey. It's a guarantee rooted in the teachings of Jesus, who made it clear that those who authentically express their faith will encounter opposition and hatred from the world.

The bottom line is this. The absence of criticism might imply a reluctance to boldly declare one's faith or a hesitancy to embody the principles outlined in the Word of God. However, taking a firm stand on our beliefs aligns with the biblical promise that living out our faith will inevitably lead to a position of opposition within the world.

A Friend Of God

People ask me how I came to believe strongly in the faith like I do. Each time, I tell them the same thing. I seek the heart of the Father, and I hang around with people who seek after the heart of the Father. I read and study the Bible, and I read books from people who read and study the Bible. I call it the trash can principle. We put garbage in the trash can. When we take it out to dump it, trash comes out. Garbage in, garbage out. If I want to be a Godly man, I don't read garbage, and I don't hang with people who treat their minds and lives like garbage cans.

The divine directive beckons us to engage in fellowship with those who have aligned themselves as friends of God. In so doing, this fellowship with fellow friends of God presents an unparalleled privilege. When God called Abraham His friend, I regarded that honor as the highlight of one's life. But just how does such a friendship come about? Delving into the dynamics of such a profound friendship prompts an exploration of the insights shared by Jesus in Luke 11:23.

Luke 11:23 (ESV) Whoever is not with me is against me, and whoever does not gather with me scatters.

The bottom line is this.

Come Out From Among Them

Chapter 3

Choose Either God or "Not God"

The recurring metaphor of spiritual light and darkness is central to understanding this connection. It necessitates perceiving the world through the lens of a polarized or contradictory opinion between those who stand in unity with Jesus and those who oppose Him. No intermediary space or middle ground exists. The world is distinctly divided into two realms, making it imperative to recognize one's stance in relation to Jesus. *There is God, and there is "not God." "There are those who walk with Him in obedience, and there are those who oppose Him openly or through compromise."*

> *John 6:66-68 (ESV) After this many of his disciples turned back and no longer walked with him. 67 So Jesus said to the twelve, "Do you want to go away as well?" 68 Simon Peter answered him, "Lord, to whom shall we go? You have the words of eternal life,*

The profound significance lies in acknowledging that the world is not characterized by shades of neutrality; instead, it is starkly divided between alignment with Jesus and His Word or opposition against Him. This perspective calls individuals to assess their positioning in this spiritual dichotomy, emphasizing the profound impact it has on the formation of a genuine friendship with God. The path to being a friend of God involves consciously aligning oneself with God's Word and purpose and recognizing the distinct realms of allegiance in His kingdom.

The Two Kingdoms

The spiritual landscape is defined by the existence of two distinct realms – the kingdom of God and the kingdom of darkness. In comprehending these realms, it's essential to recognize the elements that define a kingdom. A kingdom must have a sovereign ruler, a citizenry, a territory, a set of governing laws, and a justice system to punish rebels. These components collectively shape the character and function of a kingdom.

> *Matthew 12:26 (ESV) And if Satan casts out Satan, he is divided against himself. How then will **his kingdom stand**?*

> *2 Corinthians 4:4 (ESV) In their case **the god of this world** has blinded the minds of the unbelievers, to keep them from seeing the light of the gospel of the glory of Christ, who is the image of God.*

The point of difficulty of our daily choices lies in the conscious decision to navigate life as individuals who identify with and align themselves as children of the kingdom of God. We are influenced and pulled by the kingdom of darkness each day, often without our knowledge. The choice to embrace the kingdom of God extends beyond mere acknowledgment. It involves an ongoing commitment to live in accordance with the principles and values inherent in God's kingdom. The daily decision to walk as citizens of the kingdom of God signifies an intentional and deliberate choice to embrace the sovereignty of God. To do so means to adhere to His laws and actively participate in the spiritual inheritance of His kingdom. This defines us as friends of God.

This recognition invites individuals to embrace their role as citizens within the kingdom of God. With citizenship, one should have a profound understanding that daily choices and actions contribute to the ongoing manifestation of God's spiritual reality on earth. It's a continual commitment to aligning one's life with the principles of the kingdom of God, forging a path that reflects the sovereignty, characteristics, grace, and commands of our heavenly Father.

Entry Into The Kingdom Of God

The entry into the kingdom of God is not a casual affiliation but a profound citizenship acquired through the sacrificial shedding of blood by our Lord Jesus Christ. The purchase of our citizenship is rooted in the redemptive act of Christ, symbolized by His shed blood on the cross. This acquisition, though freely offered, is realized and made personal through the active appropriation of it by faith.

> *John 3:16 (ESV) "For God so loved the world, that he gave his only Son, that **whoever believes in him** should not perish but have eternal life.*

> *Romans 10:9-10 (ESV) because, if you **confess with your mouth that Jesus is Lord** and **believe in your heart that God raised him from the dead**, you will be saved. 10 For with the heart one believes and is justified, and with the mouth one confesses and is saved.*

Our action of faith becomes the conduit through which the benefits of this purchased citizenship are actualized in our lives. Biblical faith involves a deep and unwavering trust in the power of God through the Person of the Holy Spirit to produce the desired result of Christ's sacrifice and resurrection in us. We are to acknowledge and testify of the transformative and redemptive power in us that grants us entry into the kingdom of God. The redemptive process of spiritual adoption is not passive. Salvation requires an intentional and heartfelt embracing of the truth that our citizenship, obtained at the cost of Christ's blood, is secured through the active engagement of our faith.

Essentially, our story unfolds at redemption, where the shedding of Christ's blood becomes the currency that secures our citizenship. Our faith then serves as the key to access and experience the privileges, rights, and responsibilities inherent in being citizens of the kingdom of God.

Salvation Over The Adamic Nature

The inherent sinful nature inherited from Adam, along with the habitual sinful behaviors of humanity, establishes a state of enmity and hostility between individuals and God. The Adamic nature each of us was born with alienates us from the awesome presence of a holy God. This estrangement is characterized by a profound gulf, a stark separation, between the fallen nature of sinful humanity and the divine holiness of God. This chasm represents the natural disconnect caused by human sinfulness.

> *Romans 5:12 (ESV) Therefore, just as sin came into the world through one man, and death through sin, and so death spread to all men because all sinned—*

God's redemptive plan takes the transformative and comprehensive work of our Lord Jesus Christ in and through us. Humanity cannot save themselves, and Jesus must be seen as the only way into the kingdom of God. The bridge over this formidable gulf of sin and judgment is constructed through our Lord's virgin birth, sacrificial death, burial, resurrection, and ascension. The entirety of Christ's redemptive journey serves as the means by which the separation between a holy God and a sinful man is overcome. Faith in the finished work of the cross paved the way, and our Lord became the doorway to reconciliation between sinful humanity and a holy God.

> *John 14:6 (ESV) Jesus said to him, "I am the way, and the truth, and the life. **No one comes to the Father except through me**.*

> *Romans 5:8-10 (ESV) but God shows his love for us in that while we were still sinners, **Christ died for us**. 9 Since, therefore, **we have now been justified by his blood**, much more shall we be saved by him from the wrath of God. 10 For if while we were enemies we were reconciled to God by the death of his Son, much more, **now that we are reconciled, shall we be saved by his life.***

The crucial transition from the kingdom of darkness to the kingdom of God occurs through being born again. Each of us must experience a spiritual rebirth attained by accepting and embracing the completed work of Christ on the cross. This metamorphosis marks a profound change in status, transitioning from a state of enmity with God to a position of restored relationship and alignment with divine purposes.

> Colossians 1:13-14 (ESV) **He has delivered us from the domain of darkness** and **transferred us to the kingdom of his beloved Son**, 14 in whom we have redemption, the forgiveness of sins.

Our Relationship & Fellowship With The World Has Changed

This newfound alignment with God also entails a shift in relationships with the world and those who are spiritually lost. True born-again believers, having embraced the finished work of Christ, now find themselves at odds with the values and pursuits of the world. Those who harbor affection for the world or its allurements are consequently deemed enemies of God. Allegiance to God positions believers in opposition to the world, reinforcing the transformative impact of embracing the redemptive work of Christ.

> James 4:4 (ESV) You adulterous people! Do you not know that **friendship with the world is enmity with God**? Therefore **whoever wishes to be a friend of the world makes himself an enemy of God**.

Therefore, a genuine Biblical friend, as defined in the spiritual context, is an individual who has experienced salvation and consistently lives in alignment with the Holy Spirit, engaging in a daily walk with the Father as prescribed in His Word. This friendship is not predicated on attempting salvation attained through good works. Instead, it is a salvation that actively operates and manifests itself in one's life through faith in the life, death, and resurrection of our Lord Jesus Christ.

Not Just Hearers, But Doers Of The Word

The imperative lies in hearing the Word, actively embodying its teachings, and becoming doers of the Word. The essence of this salvation is rooted in faith, a dynamic and living faith that finds expression through our actions and deeds. It is a salvation characterized by a faith that works, encapsulating the true essence of a life lived in accordance with the principles laid out in God's Word. In other words, we do not embrace a faith that sticks its head in the sand while singing, "Que sera, sera, Whatever will be, will be." True Biblical faith is not afraid to stand on the precepts and principles of God's Word and let the chips fall where they fall.

This profound truth finds evidence in the story of Abraham, as conveyed in the Scriptures. Abraham's life serves as a testament to the inseparable connection between faith and works. It is a paradigm of living faith that is not confined to mere systematic beliefs but a faith that actively shapes one's conduct and choices. The call, therefore, is to embrace salvation by faith in Jesus Christ that intertwines with a life marked by transformative actions and obedience to the divine precepts found in the Scriptures.

> *James 1:22-25 (ESV) But be doers of the word, and not hearers only, deceiving yourselves. 23 For if anyone is a hearer of the word and not a doer, he is like a man who looks intently at his natural face in a*

> mirror. 24 For he looks at himself and goes away and at once forgets what he was like. 25 But the one who looks into the perfect law, the law of liberty, and perseveres, being no hearer who forgets but a doer who acts, he will be blessed in his doing.

> James 2:21-23 (ESV) Was not Abraham our father justified by works when he offered up his son Isaac on the altar? 22 You see that faith was active along with his works, and faith was completed by his works; 23 and the Scripture was fulfilled that says, "Abraham believed God, and it was counted to him as righteousness"—and he was called a friend of God.

Who Is Our True Family?

Our Lord provided a clear definition of who constitutes His family and friends. This is not a time to get emotional and cast off the truth of God's Word because it doesn't "feel good" to you. As I often say in my daily devotions, "It is time to put your big-boy pants on now.

Let's see who our Lord called family. These cherished relationships extend beyond mere acknowledgment of salvation; they encompass individuals actively engaged in fulfilling the will of the Father. Attempting to maintain a simultaneous connection with Jesus while entangling oneself in worldly pursuits falls short of aligning with the Father's will.

The directive is firmly rooted in the principle articulated by our Lord – a declaration that genuine love for Him is inherently linked to obedience. To claim a love for Jesus is to commit to obeying His teachings and aligning one's life with the divine will. Those considered family and friends of the Lord hinge on this commitment to actively live out the Father's will. This definition of family certainly exceeds those who embrace a superficial adherence to faith.

The bottom line is this. The call of the Father is not merely to profess salvation but to engage in a transformative journey that involves wholehearted obedience to Jesus and a conscious effort to fulfill the Father's divine purpose. This understanding redefines the nature of our relationship and fellowship with the Lord. We see that emphasizing true companionship with Christ is intricately woven with a commitment to walking in His will and obediently following His teachings. Basically, it is abandoning passive Christianity.

> *Matthew 12:46-50 (ESV) While he was still speaking to the people, behold, his mother and his brothers stood outside, asking to speak to him. 48 But he replied to the man who told him, "Who is my mother, and who are my brothers?" 49 And stretching out his hand toward his disciples, he said, "Here are my mother and my brothers! 50 For whoever does the will of my Father in heaven is my brother and sister and mother."*

> *John 15:13-15 (ESV) Greater love has no one than this, that someone lay down his life for his friends. 14 You are my friends if you do what I command you. 15 No longer do I call you servants, for the servant does not know what his master is doing; but I have called you friends, for all that I have heard from my Father I have made known to you.*

> John 14:15 (ESV) *"If you love me, you will keep my commandments.*

Where He Leads, I Will Follow

A transformative process unfolds as we dedicate our lives to the profound journey with our Lord Jesus Christ. This journey involves a daily surrendering of our desires and ways, allowing a life characterized by faith to produce good works naturally.

> *Philippians 2:13 (ESV) for it is God who works in you, both to will and to work for his good pleasure.*

The outflow of godly and humanitarian deeds flows from a faith-filled walk with Jesus, described in the children's song many years ago.

> It's bubbling, it's bubbling,
> It's bubbling in my soul.
> There's singing and laughing,
> Since Jesus made me whole.
> Folks don't understand it,
> Nor can I keep it quiet.
> But it's bubbling, bubbling, bubbling, bubbling,
> Bubbling, day and night.

We Reap What We Sow

The understanding emerges that all goodness, all virtuous endeavors, originate from the Father and are bestowed upon those who demonstrate faithfulness. This faithfulness is not merely a passive adherence but an active engagement in living out the principles and values ingrained in the character of God. Committing to faithful living becomes a conduit for receiving the gifts flowing from the Father. We reap what we sowed. We reap more than we sowed, and we reap later than we sowed.

> *James 1:17-18 (ESV) Every good gift and every perfect gift is from above, coming down from the Father of lights, with whom there is no variation or shadow due to change. 18 Of his own will he brought us forth by the word of truth, that we should be a kind of firstfruits of his creatures.*

Abiding In Christ

The essence of this journey is expressed in the concept of abiding – a continuous and intimate connection with the life of our Lord. This involves a harmonious intertwining with God's Word, wherein the principles and teachings guide our thoughts, actions, and character. The journey is one of constant learning, growth, and alignment with our heavenly Father. In Him, we foster a life that radiates His goodness that faithfully reflects the transformative power of abiding in the presence of our Lord.

> *John 15:5-7 (ESV) I am the vine; you are the branches. Whoever abides in me and I in him, he it is that bears much fruit, for apart from me you can do nothing. 6 If anyone does not abide in me he is thrown away like a branch and withers; and the branches are gathered, thrown into the fire, and burned. 7 If you abide in me, and my words abide in you, ask whatever you wish, and it will be done for you.*

There we have it. Herein lies a profound truth. True *friendship* with God is intricately bound to a relationship with Jesus Christ, coupled with an ongoing commitment to walk in fellowship with Him and the Holy Spirit. To know Jesus is to intimately acquaint oneself with both the Father and the Holy Spirit. This communion involves a dynamic exchange, encompassing speaking and listening to God, commonly called "prayer."

It's essential to recognize that God's desire to communicate with us surpasses our eagerness to listen. The Christian journey unfolds as a series of choices and priorities. The proximity of our relationship with God is a direct reflection of our choices. At this very moment, our closeness to God is contingent on the depth of our genuine desire to be close to Him. In other words, we are as close to God as we really want to be. It goes beyond verbal confessions; our actual closeness is determined by the earnestness of our hearts.

Making Choices

Our choices, influenced by our thoughts and emotions, are pivotal in shaping our fellowship with the Father. If our focus is entangled with worldly concerns, our choices will inevitably follow suit. Conversely, if our thoughts and emotions are anchored in our heavenly Father and the pursuits of His kingdom, our choices will align accordingly. We must set our minds on heavenly things. We are not to sacrifice the eternal on the altar of the temporary.

> *Colossians 3:2-8 (ESV) Set your minds on things that are above, not on things that are on earth. 3 For you have died, and your life is hidden with Christ in God. 4*

Come Out From Among Them

When Christ who is your life appears, then you also will appear with him in glory. 5 Put to death therefore what is earthly in you: sexual immorality, impurity, passion, evil desire, and covetousness, which is idolatry. 6 On account of these the wrath of God is coming. 7 In these you too once walked, when you were living in them. 8 But now you must put them all away: anger, wrath, malice, slander, and obscene talk from your mouth.

Philippians 4:8 (ESV) Finally, brothers, whatever is true, whatever is honorable, whatever is just, whatever is pure, whatever is lovely, whatever is commendable, if there is any excellence, if there is anything worthy of praise, think about these things.

Ephesians 4:22-24 (ESV) to put off your old self, which belongs to your former manner of life and is corrupt through deceitful desires, 23 and to be renewed in the spirit of your minds, 24 and to put on the new self, created after the likeness of God in true righteousness and holiness.

Let's be honest with ourselves and confront our sincerity. The reality is that we are either God's friend or God's enemy. If we are God's enemy, we are spiritually lost or a believer who is in love with the world and walking in unrepentant sin. If we are God's friend, we are saved and walking in obedience to His Word and the anointing of the Holy Spirit. If we are God's friend, we carry great responsibilities concerning guarding our hearts from those who are not His friends.

Even as God's children, redeemed by the blood of the Lamb, we have the capacity to act in ways that mimic enmity toward the Father and the work of the cross of our Lord. The challenge lies in aligning our choices with the profound truth of our identity as God's friends and children, steering clear of behaviors contradicting our divine position as a child of the King.

> *Romans 5:10 (ESV) For if while we were enemies we were reconciled to God by the death of his Son, much more, now that we are reconciled, shall we be saved by his life.*

The bottom line is this.
Be a friend of God, and as for our enemies,

Come Out From Among Them

Chapter 4

Avoid Unruly Christians
Romans 16:17-18

Understanding God's command to love our fellow Christian brothers and sisters is essential. Yet, there are instances where our interpretation of love might lead us to believe that unity and fellowship should be maintained with everyone, especially within the Christian community. However, Scriptural guidance indicates otherwise. The Scriptures direct us to exercise discernment, particularly when Christians deviate from Christ-like behavior and refuse to repent. In such cases, separation becomes a necessary course of action.

Furthermore, if Christians begin to propagate doctrines that contradict the teachings of Jesus and the apostles, mere association becomes dangerous. Religious titles such as "pastor" or "teacher" do not automatically warrant fellowship. It is disconcerting to encounter numerous pastors with messages rooted in social, psychological, or self-help themes rather than a foundation in the Biblical gospel. Identifying a building as a church does not obligate us to fellowship with its congregation. Many churches today espouse a universal doctrine suggesting that Jesus is merely "a way" to God, not "the way." Such a doctrine is considered heretical, and the Scriptures advise disassociation from such beliefs. In other words, we are to come out from among them.

Although adhering to these principles may strain some relationships due to emotional bonds, obedience to the Scriptures must take precedence. The Apostle Paul's counsel urges us to separate ourselves from Christian brothers displaying unruly or disorderly conduct in both speech and action. This separation may extend to distancing ourselves from an individual or even an entire corporate body of believers.

Romans 16:17-18

In this study, we will let the Bible interpret the Bible. If you are emotionally driven, then you won't care what the Bible says because your mind is already made up as to what you will do because it feels right. For those who are still teachable and desire to learn God's Word, even if we are offended by it, I will break each verse down and give the Greek texts.

Romans 16:17 (ESV) I appeal to you, brothers, to <u>watch out</u> for those <u>who cause</u> divisions and create obstacles contrary to the doctrine that you have been taught; avoid them.

In accordance with Romans 16:17-18, believers are instructed to remain vigilant for individuals who sow discord, create obstacles, or introduce stumbling blocks within the Christian community. The term "watch" is derived from the Greek word **"skopeo,"** signifying an active and intentional stance. It encompasses actions such as taking aim, vigilant observation, heeding, marking, fixing one's eyes on, and directing attention toward potentially divisive elements. This directive implies a proactive engagement rather than a passive or indifferent posture. The call is to actively and purposefully monitor the environment, identifying and addressing any factors that may lead to division or create obstacles within the Christian community.

In Romans 16:17-18, individuals who warrant separation are those found guilty of causing division and introducing obstacles within the community of believers. The term "guilty" here refers to their actions that disrupt the unity and hinder the smooth functioning of the faith community.

This may encompass behaviors such as promoting divisive doctrines, fostering discord among believers, or creating impediments to collective spiritual growth. The criteria for separation are rooted in the observed actions of the individual that go against the Christian principles of harmony, mutual support, and the overall well-being of the Christian community. Therefore, those mentioned in Romans 16:17-18 are guilty of actions that undermine the cohesion and spiritual progress of the fellowship, prompting the need for separation from such disruptive influences.

Romans 16:17 (ESV) I appeal to you, brothers, to watch out for those who cause divisions and create obstacles contrary to the doctrine that you have been taught; <u>avoid them.</u>

The term "avoid" in the context of the Greek word **"ekklino"** carries a detailed meaning. This word encompasses various actions, including deviating from a particular path, actively shunning, consciously going out of one's way to avoid contact, turning aside from a given course, and deliberately turning away from a specific direction.

The multifaceted nature of **"ekklino"** implies comprehensive and intentional avoidance, emphasizing a physical departure from a particular route or person and a mental and emotional distancing. It conveys the idea of purposefully steering clear of something or someone, signifying a deliberate choice to disengage or separate oneself from a particular influence or situation.

Romans 16:18 (ESV) <u>For such persons do not serve our Lord Christ</u>, but their own appetites, and by smooth talk and flattery they deceive the hearts of the naive.

We see in Romans 16 that the Apostle Paul is addressing Christian individuals characterized by self-serving tendencies with the primary focus on satisfying their personal desires in life. These fall into a specific category within the church.

I advocate for recognizing three distinct groups, commonly called the three "Cs" in the church: the *Consumers*, the *Critics*, and the *Contributors*. I also call these three groups *the takers, the keepers, and the givers.* In the context of Romans 16:17-18, Paul addresses the issue of *Consumers*—individuals who are part of the church body solely for the purpose of fulfilling their own needs and desires.

These individuals contribute little or nothing to the communal dynamics of the church; their presence is primarily marked by a self-centered orientation, bringing to the table only their appetites without actively contributing to the collective well-being of the church community. They add to the Christian community division while creating obstacles contrary to sound Biblical doctrine

The bottom line is this.
Come Out From Among Them

Chapter 5

Keep Away From Unruly Christians
2 Thessalonians 3:6
Part 1

Let us delve into the insights provided by the Apostle Paul regarding these particular unruly believers within the Thessalonian church. Now, let's dissect the verse for our edification.

2 Thessalonians 3:6 (ESV) <u>Now we command you,</u> brothers, in the name of our Lord Jesus Christ, that you keep away from any brother who is walking in idleness and not in accord with the tradition that you received from us.

To gain a comprehensive understanding of 2 Thessalonians 3:6, it's crucial to examine the entire passage within its context, from 2 Thessalonians 3:6-12. Notably, the use of strong and authoritative language in the form of a command becomes evident.

2 Thessalonians 3:6 (ESV) Now we command you, brothers, <u>in the name of our Lord Jesus Christ</u>, that you keep away from any brother who is walking in idleness and not in accord with the tradition that you received from us.

In praying for the sick, meeting personal needs, or engaging in spiritual warfare, invoking the name of our

Lord Jesus Christ is a common thread. This name holds inherent power and authority. In the specific context of 2 Thessalonians 3, Paul imparts a message of paramount importance, compelling him to employ the authoritative name of our Lord Jesus Christ within the command.

The gravity of Paul's directive is evident. This passage of Scripture not only carries the weight of command but is further reinforced by the profound authority vested in the name of our Lord Jesus Christ. The entirety of the kingdom's governance under our Lord aligns with and supports this command to keep away from certain Christian brothers. Think about this. All of the kingdom government of our Lord stands behind this command.

So, what is the command at the heart of this matter? It is a directive to distance oneself from Christian brothers who lead a life of idleness, deviating from the teachings imparted by Paul. The strength of this command is not merely in its issuance. Still, it is amplified by the authority vested in the name of our Lord Jesus Christ, symbolizing a directive backed by the entirety of the divine government of the kingdom of heaven.

2 Thessalonians 3:6 (ESV) Now we command you, <u>brothers,</u> in the name of our Lord Jesus Christ, that you keep away from <u>any brother</u> who is walking in idleness and not in accord with the tradition that you received from us.

In this particular passage, Paul adopts a direct and unequivocal approach, leaving no room for a situation in which the meaning may cause confusion. He emphasizes the imperative of impartiality, disallowing any favoritism or preference among Christian believers. The directive is clear: any unruly behavior exhibited by a brother in Christ demands attention.

The term "brother," as used in this context, extends beyond natural or civil relationships. Paul does not refer to family ties, neighborhood acquaintances, or individuals from the same geographical location. Instead, he employs the term in an ecclesiastical sense, denoting someone recognized as a brother due to their status as a child of God – one who has embraced the Lord Jesus Christ as their Savior. In Paul's perspective, judgment is not cast upon those outside the realm of Christ; rather, it is reserved for those within the church, specifically believers.

This distinction underscores the gravity of accountability within the community of believers. Paul asserts the responsibility to address and confront unruly behavior among those who have embraced the Lord Jesus Christ, highlighting the distinct nature of the relationships and judgments within the ecclesiastical realm. We are not to judge those outside the church or the spiritually lost. But we have a direct command to judge (evaluate and assess) those with the church or the spiritually saved.

> *1 Corinthians 5:12-13 (ESV) For what have I to do with judging outsiders? Is it not those inside the church whom you are to judge? 13 God judges those outside. "Purge the evil person from among you."*

Come Out From Among Them

2 Thessalonians 3:6 (ESV) Now we command you, brothers, in the name of our Lord Jesus Christ, <u>that you keep away from any brother</u> who is walking in idleness and not in accord with the tradition that you received from us.

The directive is clear: we are instructed to discontinue fellowship with individuals who display unruly behavior. We are not to stop loving them but to love them from a distance. When comparing Paul's warnings in 1 Thessalonians 4:11 and 5:14 with 2 Thessalonians 3:6, the difference lies in the severity of the tone.

1 Thessalonians 4:11 (ESV) and to aspire to live quietly, and to mind your own affairs, and to work with your hands, as we instructed you,

1 Thessalonians 5:14 (ESV) And we urge you, brothers, admonish the idle, encourage the fainthearted, help the weak, be patient with them all.

In 2 Thessalonians 3:6, the apostle adopts a much sterner language, indicating an escalation in the urgency of the matter since writing his first letter to the church. Despite Paul's initial warning in his first letter to the Thessalonians, the issue of unruliness persisted. Consequently, he now advises the community to take decisive action by disciplining the unruly members, urging their separation from the fellowship.

Examining the language used in 2 Thessalonians 3:6, the phrase "keep away from" or "withdraw yourselves" is derived from the Greek word **"stello."** This term signifies abstaining from associating, removing oneself, and departing. Importantly, the withdrawal is not based on failure to conform to human traditions but is rooted in the apostolic tradition and teachings found in God's Word.

The purpose behind withdrawing from disobedient Christians is not primarily punitive; rather, it aims to deny these individuals the support, joy, and comfort of fellowship within the body of Christ. This separation is intended to endure until repentance occurs, signifying a genuine change in mindset, conversation, and actions. By placing worldly-minded Christians outside the church and into the domain of the demonic, the hope is that they might recognize their absence from the fellowship, leading them to repent of their disobedience, divisiveness, and false doctrines

It's crucial to note that such separation is reserved for cases of disorderly conduct. Not every transgression warrants this level of response, as all individuals are prone to moments of sin. Paul emphasizes that believers are not to be judged harshly for occasional disorders, nor should they judge others with such severity for a single transgression. As long as we are in the flesh or the body, we will have moments of sin and offenses of God's Word. Therefore, we are not to be judged by this harshly, nor are we to judge other believers harshly for a single disorder.

The bottom line is this.
Come Out From Among Them

Chapter 6

Keep Away From Unruly Christians
2 Thessalonians 3:6
Part 2

2 Thessalonians 3:6 (ESV) Now we command you, brothers, in the name of our Lord Jesus Christ, that you keep away from any brother <u>who is walking in idleness</u> and not in accord with the tradition that you received from us.

In this context, the term "idleness" signifies more than a mere lack of activity; it points to a disorderly manner of living that deviates from the prescribed order laid out in God's Word. Individuals characterized by idleness are those Christians who, regardless of the teachings from the Scriptures, choose to march to the beat of their own drum.

Their vision for life is predominantly worldly, and they exhibit greater enthusiasm for indulging in worldly pleasures than adhering to the precepts and disciplines outlined in God's Word. Despite being saved, their devotion and fellowship do not align with the Word of God and the community of believers.

In response to such behavior, the Scriptural command is clear – believers are directed to withdraw themselves and abstain from fellowship with these individuals. It's crucial to note that this directive doesn't diminish our love for them but implies a commanded love from a distance. We can love without fellowshipping or communing together. For example, we should love our enemies but not walk with them. (Psalms 1).

A key distinction lies in understanding there is a difference between being guilty of a disorder or a sinful act and actively walking in a disorderly manner. To walk disorderly denotes a continuous course of life marked by a series of unruly behaviors. These believers persist in a progressive pattern that leads to increased ungodliness. Due to their affinity for the world over the Word of God, they find pleasure in their disorders. Their failure to recognize their sins stems from deliberately choosing to follow their own ways, delighting in doing what seems right in their own eyes.

I know the easy way out for many Christians is to brand these people as lost church members. However, we would have to correct the Apostle Paul in his dealings with the church of Corinth in their crazy behavior. In all their immoral and immature behavior, Paul still addressed them as believers.

This passage in 2 Thessalonians 3:6 echoes similar sentiments found in 1 Thessalonians 4:11 and 5:14. In his first letter to the church, Paul had already identified a disposition towards idleness and unruliness among some members. In response, he tenderly exhorted them to be quiet, mind their own business, and engage in productive work. The warnings in 1 Thessalonians served as initial instructions for addressing the issue of idleness and disorderliness within the church.

Come Out From Among Them

> *1 Thessalonians 4:11-12 (ESV) and to aspire to live quietly, and **to mind your own affairs**, and to work with your hands, as we instructed you, 12 so that you may walk properly before outsiders and be dependent on no one.*

> *1 Thessalonians 5:14 (ESV) And we urge you, brothers, **admonish the idle**, encourage the fainthearted, help the weak, be patient with them all.*

We scratched the surface earlier, but now let's dig deeper into 2 Thessalonians 3:6. Within the framework of 2 Thessalonians 3:6, the expression "who is walking" extends beyond the realm of mere physical motion; it denotes a full engagement with life, a meticulous governance of one's behavior, and a purposeful mode of existence. The Greek tense associated with "walks" conveys conduct that is not an occasional judgment error but a deliberate, conscious, and enduring way of life. Individuals characterized as disorderly exemplify a persistent pattern of unruliness ingrained into their lifestyle.

In this context, being unruly means behaving as if one is entirely independent, isolated like an island, and guided solely by personal discretion or whims. This self-centered approach leaves no room for considering the church community as a cohesive whole.

The metaphor employed here draws from a military context, suggesting that every individual has a designated post or position in life and within the Church. Each person is expected to be present at their assigned post, fulfilling their role rather than being absent or deviating from it. The analogy teaches us that every member is crucial within the body of Christ, with unique functions that cannot be fulfilled by anyone else.

Regrettably, some individuals within the body of Christ exhibit an "Absent Without Leave" (A.W.O.L.) attitude, neglecting their responsibilities and roles within the Christian community. The essence of being part of a larger whole, an integral member of an organic body, is emphasized. Each member is entrusted with specific functions that contribute to the body's overall well-being, and these responsibilities cannot be overlooked or dismissed without consequence.

2 Thessalonians 3:6 (ESV) Now we command you, brothers, in the name of our Lord Jesus Christ, that you keep away from any brother who is walking in idleness <u>and not in accord with the tradition that you received from us.</u>

In 2 Thessalonians 3:6, the question arises: What actions render individuals guilty and necessitate our separation from them? Paul categorizes the disorderly as those who deviate from the oral and written traditions passed down by Paul and the apostles. In essence, these individuals reject obedience to the Word of God both in their spoken words and their actions. This stands in stark contrast to the exemplary conduct of the early believers depicted in the book of Acts.

> *Acts 2:41-42 (ESV) So those who received his word were baptized, and there were added that day about three thousand souls. 42 And they devoted*

themselves to the apostles' teaching and the fellowship, to the breaking of bread and the prayers.

Therefore, based on the teaching of Romans 16:17-18 and 2 Thessalonians 3:6 concerning Christians who cause divisions, create obstacles, walk in idleness, and disobey sound doctrine, what are we to do? We are to love them, but we are to keep away from them and avoid them.

The bottom line is this.

Come Out From Among Them

Chapter 7

Have Nothing To Do With Unruly Christians
2 Thessalonians 3:14-15 &
Titus 3:10-11

Paul provides additional examples in 2 Thessalonians 3:14-15, instructing believers to take note of and mark those individuals, having no further association with them. Despite this separation, the underlying principle is love – love for God and obedience to His Word. It doesn't signify a lack of love for the separated individuals but prioritizes love for God and adherence to His commands.

2 Thessalonians 3:14-15 (ESV) If anyone does not obey what we say in this letter, <u>take note of that person, and have nothing to do with him,</u> that he may be ashamed. 15 Do not regard him as an enemy, but warn him as a brother.

Paul is an example for believers to follow, illustrating his approach between the first and second letters to the Thessalonians when addressing the issue of unruly behavior among the brethren. In Titus 3:10-11, Paul provides a clear directive to Titus regarding those causing division. He advises Titus to issue one or two warnings to such individuals and subsequently to disassociate from them. In essence, the directive implies a love that maintains a certain distance – an affectionate separation, as believers are directed to cease fellowship with those causing division.

Titus 3:10-11 (ESV) As for <u>a person who stirs up division</u>, after <u>warning him once and then twice</u>, <u>have nothing more to do with him</u>, 11 knowing that such a person is warped and sinful; he is self-condemned.

This course of action is not a disavowal of love but a demonstration of love from a relational distance. The decision to cease fellowship is driven by a commitment to follow Paul's guidance and maintain the integrity of the community. Remember, these are not Paul's words. He spoke under the inspiration of the Holy Spirit, the words of God the Father. Importantly, Paul's actions align with the principles he imparts, reinforcing the seriousness of the matter at hand. The emphasis is on holding individuals accountable for their divisive behavior and, when necessary, creating a relational boundary to protect the unity and well-being of the Christian community.

The bottom line is this.

Come Out From Among Them

Chapter 8

Do Not Associate With Unruly Christians
1 Corinthians 5:9-13
Part 1

Many mainline denominational churches face a demographic shift characterized by an aging membership. This phenomenon is accompanied by a decline in attendance and a noticeable increase in the average age of church members. In response to these dynamics, churches find themselves eager to extend warm welcomes to anyone entering their doors.

While the foundational principle of loving all people is emphasized, a subtle difference or distinction exists. Their sense of obligation to love everyone causes them to embrace all Christian brothers and sisters. They also warmly welcome spiritual enemies, similar to the greetings reserved for our fellow believers. We must recognize this broad love mandate does not mean we offer indiscriminate fellowship to all individuals. The Scriptures provide guidance on discerning those with whom believers are called to walk in harmony and those from whom they are instructed to distance themselves.

To delve into this matter, it is instructive to turn to the words of the Apostle Paul in 1 Corinthians 5:9-13, where he issues specific commands regarding the company believers should keep and those from whom they should maintain a necessary separation. Again, I should warn the reader to allow the Scriptures to speak for themselves and not to interpret the Scriptures through their emotions.

1 Corinthians 5:9-13

1 Corinthians 5:9-13 (ESV) I wrote to you in my letter <u>not to associate with</u> sexually immoral people— 10 not at all meaning the sexually immoral of this world, or the greedy and swindlers, or idolaters, since then you would need to go out of the world. 11 But now I am writing to you <u>not to associate with anyone who bears the name of brother</u> if he is guilty of sexual immorality or greed, or is an idolater, reviler, drunkard, or swindler—<u>not even to eat with such a one</u>. 12 For what have I to do with judging outsiders? <u>Is it not those inside the church whom you are to judge?</u> 13 God judges those outside. <u>"Purge the evil person from among you."</u>

Let's look at the verse line by line. But Remember!

The bottom line is this.

Come Out From Among Them

Chapter 9

Do Not Associate With Unruly Christians
1 Corinthians 5:9
Part 2

1 Corinthians 5:9 (ESV) <u>I wrote to you in my letter</u> not to associate with sexually immoral people—

This statement suggests that the apostle Paul maintained regular communication with the Corinthian church even before the two letters that are currently present in the Scriptures. The implication raises questions about the possibility of lost Biblical letters that might be concealed somewhere. Could there be missing parts of what was intended to be part of the Bible and possibly destroyed over time? No! The fact remains that God, in His divine wisdom, designated these specific two letters as inspired and deemed them fit for inclusion in His sacred book known as the Bible. The assurance is given that nothing divinely inspired has been lost over time.

> *Isaiah 40:8 (ESV) The grass withers, the flower fades, but the word of our God will stand forever.*

> *Matthew 5:18 (ESV) For truly, I say to you, until heaven and earth pass away, not an iota, not a dot, will pass from the Law until all is accomplished.*

> *1 Peter 1:24-25 (ESV) for "All flesh is like grass and all its glory like the flower of grass. The grass withers,*

and the flower falls, 25 but the word of the Lord remains forever." And this word is the good news that was preached to you.

We must emphasize that every word, whether written or spoken by Paul, is not necessarily to be regarded as holy inspired Scriptures. Not everything Paul said was a word relayed to him from the Father. Paul had the right to communicate encouragement and correction to a church independently. These forms of communication were not esteemed as inspired by the Holy Spirit. This aspect is described as a form of teaching and discipleship.

I can give an example if you allow me a little ground for personal testimony. This example is in no way saying that the Holy Spirit inspires my words, which should be written down as Holy Writ. On Sunday morning I minister a Word that I fully believe the Father gave under the direction of the Holy Spirit from His written Word. However, my form of communication on Sunday mornings when I preach God's Word is certainly different from sitting around the table with the guys over coffee on Monday mornings. We may still get into the Word, but on Monday mornings, we can discuss different events such as politics, sports, and the economy. We also bring up "how to" projects because someone has something that needs to be repaired every week.

The conclusion drawn is that Paul engaged in the exchange of ordinary private letters. The communication between Paul and the church shifted when Paul somehow became aware of the issue of sexual immorality within the church. This prompted further communication, inspired by the Holy Spirit, and we enjoy reading and studying it through the historical context known as the Bible. We are not sure of how he received the information, but we know of Paul's prior knowledge of sexual misconduct in the church from what he said in 1 Corinthians 5:1-2.

> *1 Corinthians 5:1-2 (ESV)* **It is actually reported** *that there is sexual immorality among you, and of a kind that is not tolerated even among pagans, for a man has his father's wife. 2 And you are arrogant! Ought you not rather to mourn? Let him who has done this be removed from among you.*

The origin of the content in question is speculated to have its roots in either a letter written by Paul or information conveyed by someone who visited him during his time in prison. This leads to the deduction that the two letters, 1 and 2 Corinthians, are not the sole means of communication Paul had with the Corinthian church. While acknowledging the existence of other communications, it is asserted that these particular letters have been singled out and designated as inspired by the Holy Spirit for relevance as the Word of God included in our Bibles.

The understanding is conveyed that the Apostles, including Paul, composed numerous letters addressed to various churches, but many of these have been lost to time. These letters were considered crucial for addressing specific issues within a particular church during a specific period. However, the assertion is made that not all of these letters were inspired by the Holy Spirit to serve as enduring guidance for the entire body of believers throughout time. Consequently, the letters that were not deemed to have universal applicability were not preserved by the Holy Spirit. Now, let's continue with 1 Corinthians 5:9-13.

Come Out From Among Them

1 Corinthians 5:9 (ESV) I wrote to you in my letter <u>not to associate with sexually immoral people</u>—

The expression "not to associate with" or "not to company with" finds its linguistic origins in the Greek term "sunanamignumi." This term carries the connotation of refraining from mixing, mingling, or associating with a particular person. The depth of this meaning is observed in its usage not only in the context mentioned but also in other instances, such as Ephesians 5:11 and 2 Thessalonians 3:14.

In Ephesians 5:11 and 2 Thessalonians 3:14, the same Greek word, "sunanamignumi," is employed to convey the idea of avoiding entanglement or close association with certain elements or individuals. This linguistic consistency across different Biblical passages underscores the significance of the term and its application in guiding behavior and relationships for believers.

*Ephesians 5:11 (ESV) **<u>Take no part</u>** in the unfruitful works of darkness, but **<u>instead expose them</u>**.*

*2 Thessalonians 3:14 (ESV) If anyone does not obey what we say in this letter, **<u>take note of that person, and have nothing to do with him</u>**, that he may be ashamed.*

The bottom line is this.

Come Out From Among Them

Chapter 10

Do Not Associate With Unruly Christians
1 Corinthians 5:10
Part 3

1 Corinthians 5:10 (ESV) not at all meaning the sexually immoral of this world, <u>or the greedy and swindlers, or idolaters</u>, since then you would need to go out of the world.

Or with the covetous or the greedy denotes individuals driven by an unsatisfied desire for material gain. These individuals engage in various forms of impurity with an insatiable greed, finding no satisfaction in their unscrupulous pursuits. The term "covetous" is the relentless desire for more. Previous Scriptures have already established the warning to avoid association with such individuals.

"Extortioners" or swindlers are those who exploit their greed by oppressing the vulnerable, the poor, the needy, and the fatherless in order to amass wealth. Through force and manipulation, they violate the purity and innocence of others, stealing property, oppressing the less fortunate, and withholding wages through fraudulent means. The term describes those who resort to violent or manipulative theft.

The phrase "Or an idolater" encompasses the entire Corinthian population before the gospel was preached, as they were once idol worshippers.

In this 1 Corinthians 5:10 passage, the Apostle Paul addresses a broad spectrum of sins against fellow humans, highlighting fornication as a sin against oneself, covetousness and extortion as sins against neighbors, and idolatry as a sin against God.

1 Corinthians 5:10 (ESV) not at all meaning the sexually immoral of this world, or the greedy and swindlers, or idolaters, <u>since then you would need to go out of the world.</u>

The statement "Since then, you would need to go out of the world" is a rhetorical expression, emphasizing the impracticality and impossibility of altogether avoiding individuals of such sinful inclinations. Paul suggests that attempting to separate oneself entirely from these sins would require death or a departure from the world. The world is filled with such individuals committing such sins, making it impossible to avoid them entirely. However, they should not be in the church.

This passage underscores the inevitability of having some contact with moral or immoral lost individuals or worldly people on a daily basis. Engaging in communication and interaction as members of the social community is deemed necessary. We shop, work, and travel. There are certainly enough lost people to go around for us to come into contact with the world and their sinful ways. Paul clarifies that when he mentions avoiding association, he is not referring to non-believers in the world. Paul did not want the Corinthian Christians to expect godly behavior from ungodly people. Again, let me say he cautions against expecting godly behavior from those who do not adhere to godly principles. In other words, we should not expect lost people to act like Christians. However, we should not tolerate Christians acting like lost people. Disassociating from sinners in a sinful world would necessitate leaving the world entirely.

The Scriptures clarify the extent of communication and association we should engage with non-believers. Believers are called to come out from among them, emphasizing separation from the values and practices that contradict Biblical principles of faith.

Romans 12:2 (KJV) And be not conformed to this world: but be ye transformed by the renewing of your mind, that ye may prove what is that good, and acceptable, and perfect, will of God.

The guiding principles regarding communication and association are clear: we are to spread the gospel message, demonstrating kindness to others as neighbors and fellow members of the Christian community. A fundamental command directs believers to uphold justice in all transactions with those outside the faith.

While engagement in business transactions and education with non-believers is permitted, the primary aim is to contribute positively and do them good. However, the picture is clear. There is to be no companionship or association with them in their wickedness, whether as idolaters, covetous individuals, or those given to licentious behavior. Believers are cautioned against being identified as participants in such ungodly practices.

The foundational understanding is that as believers, we are called holy and set apart for the Lord. This sanctification necessitates separation from those who are not aligned with these principles. The command to be separate implies abstaining from intimate association with the spiritually lost or believers walking in unconfessed sins.

Maintaining this separation is not solely for the preservation of one's own character but also to prevent corruption, as shown by the examples of non-believers. It is a precaution against being led astray by their conduct, which may potentially lead to neglecting vital spiritual disciplines such as prayer and participation in the sanctuary with other saints.

In this journey, believers are reminded of the obligation to engage in acts of charity and extend goodwill to others by sharing the transformative message of the gospel. Believers are also to be reminded of their responsibility to love sinners but to hate their sins. The underlying caution is meant to keep Christians from adopting practices that would conform them to the worldly image. We must emphasize the importance of preserving the distinctiveness of the Biblical Christian identity. The call to remain unswervingly committed to the principles of faith and avoid actions that compromise the sanctity of the believer serves as a resounding theme throughout these Biblical mandates. Let's continue with 1 Corinthians 5:11.

Charles W Morris

The bottom line is this.
Come Out From Among Them

Chapter 11

Do Not Associate With Unruly Christians
1 Corinthians 5:11
Part 4

The reference in question pertains to individuals characterized by a specific character trait. However, Paul, in his discourse in 1 Corinthians 5:11, directs his attention towards describing or portraying the appropriate level of interaction with those individuals who are part of the church community guilty of the sins addressed.

1 Corinthians 5:11 (ESV) But now I am writing to you <u>not to associate with anyone</u> who bears the name of brother if he is guilty of sexual immorality or greed, or is an idolater, reviler, drunkard, or swindler—<u>not even to eat with such a one.</u>

Paul explicitly advises against associating with fornicators. The Greek term employed for "sexually immoral" in the text is "pornos," from which the English words "porn" and "pornography" are derived. It is a masculine term signifying a male engaged in sexual transgressions outside the bounds of marriage or a fornicator. This marks Paul's initial guidance to the church on addressing unrepentant sexual sins within their midst.

Paul's stance, which the Holy Spirit inspired, is definite. Words inspired by the Holy Spirit means they were first spoken by God the Father. Paul states there should be no sharing of meals or participating in the Lord's Supper with such individuals. The Apostle emphatically asserts that any form of association or mingling with them should be categorically avoided. He states that God declares these sins should never be tolerated within the body of Christ.

Of course, someone will bring up the woman caught in adultery. Jesus spoke and related to her. Yes. He said, go and sin no more, which should also be our message. I will remind you that Paul had warned the Corinth church of this sexual conduct in 1 Corinthians. Therefore, the "go and sin no more" option was on the table, calling the church to repent, but it was ignored.

In his communication to the Corinthians, Paul relates the potential harm of leaving sexual sins unaddressed within the church. He highlights the risk of these sins becoming stumbling blocks for weaker or less mature Christians. The unaddressed presence of such sins might allure and draw others, by way of ungodly example, onto the same sinful path. This consideration prompts Paul to emphasize the necessity of taking decisive action against unrepentant sexual sins within the church to safeguard the spiritual well-being of its members.

Notice that in 1 Corinthians 5:10, the Apostle Paul identifies that he is speaking about believers or those within the church, not those who are of the world or spiritually lost. In 1 Corinthians 5:12-13, Paul tells us we have nothing to do with judging those who are spiritually lost.

Come Out From Among Them

1 Corinthians 5:10 (ESV) not at all meaning the sexually immoral <u>of this world</u>, or the greedy and swindlers, or idolaters, since then you would need to go out of the world.

1 Corinthians 5:12-13 (ESV) For what have I to do with judging outsiders? Is it not those inside the church whom you are to judge? 13 God judges those outside. "Purge the evil person from among you."

The expression "Of this world" in 1 Corinthians 5:10 pertains to individuals outside the realm of the church, specifically those who do not identify as Christians. While recognizing and not endorsing the sins of non-believers, it is acknowledged that sin is an inherent aspect of their Adamic nature. In essence, sinners are inherently inclined toward sinful behavior. Sinners know how to sin.

Let's look at the sins Paul was addressing. Remember that Paul is not speaking about Christians in the church who fall and commit these sins once. As we have said, Paul is coming against Christians who are making these sins a lifestyle and refusing to confess or repent. There are those in the body of Christ who are ready to nail Christians to the barn door over sexual sins yet don't address other continual lifestyle sins within the church. As believers, we must be careful about the "pet sins" we target while neglecting everything else. We have previously addressed the issue of unrepentant sexual sins within the church. Let's continue with the list.

The bottom line is this.
Come Out From Among Them

Chapter 12

Do Not Associate With Unruly Christians
1 Corinthians 5:11
Part 5

1 Corinthians 5:11 (ESV) <u>**But now I am writing to you not to associate with anyone who bears the name of brother**</u> **if he is guilty of sexual immorality or greed, or is an idolater, reviler, drunkard, or swindler—not even to eat with such a one.**

The introduction of the "but now" statement suggests that Paul had previously penned personal and private letters to the church before the present one. The phrase "but now have I written unto you" implies a distinction in time and context, indicating that the prior correspondence occurred on a separate occasion and in another epistle. These earlier letters, likely serving as Paul's personal exhortations and edifications to the church, are distinguished from the present communication, which carries the weight of being under the inspiration of the Holy Spirit. The use of "but now" functions not merely as a temporal marker but rather as a transition, akin to our contemporary use of "so."

Paul communicates the reason behind his current writing, suggesting that he may have initially conveyed the message verbally, perhaps addressing issues of church discipline. This verbal communication could be likened to us discussing matters within a company verbally with its leaders. Then, to ensure they don't miscommunicate the verbal message, we return later with a written email. Now that it is written, there is no reason for it to be misunderstood.

Likewise, here in 1 Corinthians, Paul returns with a written communication to ensure clarity and prevent any miscommunication, leaving no room for misunderstanding or oversight. In a parallel manner, Paul asserts, "I have written to you," signifying his deliberate intent to provide a directive that necessitates a complete separation from someone who professes religion but engages in reprehensible conduct. The injunction is explicit - believers are not to associate with or maintain any form of connection with such an individual. This separation aligns with the divine intent of our heavenly Father, indicating a clear divine mandate to abstain from any association with such a person.

The term "Brother," in its technical sense, refers to "a Christian." It encompasses any individual, whether male or female, professing to be a follower of Christ. The essential criteria is the person's belief in our Lord Jesus Christ. Paul emphasizes the gravity of the directive by specifying that it applies not only to a brother but also to any professing Christian, stressing the universal applicability of this principle within the faith community. In 1 Corinthians 5:11, Paul tells us what to watch for, which would cause us to exclude these Christian brothers and sisters from our fellowship.

1 Corinthians 5:11 (ESV) But now I am writing to you not to associate with anyone who bears the name of brother <u>if he is guilty</u> of sexual immorality or greed, or is an idolater, reviler, drunkard, or swindler—not even to eat with such a one.

The condition of being deemed guilty in this context signifies that two credible witnesses have testified against the individual. The notion of guilt hinges on the presence of two witnesses, emphasizing the requirement for a formal charge to be supported by credible testimony rather than relying on mere hearsay or gossip transmitted from one person to another.

1 Corinthians 5:11 (ESV) But now I am writing to you not to associate with anyone who bears the name of brother if he is guilty <u>of sexual immorality</u> or greed, or is an idolater, reviler, drunkard, or swindler—not even to eat with such a one.

Illustrating this principle, 1 Corinthians 5:1 serves as our example, showcasing a documented case of confirmed sexual immorality within the church. The verse stands as a concrete example where the charge of wrongdoing is not based on unfounded rumors or casual talk. The changes are substantiated by the credible testimony of two witnesses, adhering to the scriptural standard for establishing guilt within the Christian community.

> 1 Corinthians 5:1-2 (ESV) <u>It is actually reported that there is sexual immorality among you</u>, and of a kind that is not tolerated even among pagans, for a man has his father's wife. 2 And you are arrogant! Ought

you not rather to mourn? <u>Let him who has done this be removed from among you.</u>

1 Corinthians 5:11 (ESV) But now I am writing to you not to associate with anyone who bears the name of brother if he is guilty of sexual immorality or greed, or <u>is an idolater</u>, reviler, drunkard, or swindler—not even to eat with such a one.

This statement echoes the sentiments expressed in 1 Corinthians 5:10. The phrase "Or an idolater" alludes to individuals who, despite professing Christianity, actively participated in idol feasts and engaged in worship within that context. This inference is drawn from Paul's concurrent discussion about their consumption of food dedicated to idols, indicating a direct association with idolatrous practices likely occurring at these feasts.

The gravity of disregarding this warning extends to eternal consequences. The focus here is on individuals within the body of Christ, Christians, becoming entangled in the sins explicitly outlined by Paul in 1 Corinthians 5. In Ephesians 5, Paul amplifies the severity of the matter by stating that those persisting in these sins will not inherit the kingdom of God.

This stresses the profound spiritual ramifications associated with the unrepentant activity of indulging in sexual immorality, covetousness, and idolatry. The warning serves as a piercing reminder of the need for believers to steer clear of these sins for the sake of their spiritual destiny.

Ephesians 5:3-5 (ESV) But sexual immorality and all impurity or covetousness must not even be named *among you, as is proper among saints. 4 Let there be no filthiness nor foolish talk nor crude joking, which are out of place, but instead let there be thanksgiving. 5 For you may be sure of this, that everyone who is sexually immoral or impure, or <u>who is covetous (that is, an idolater)</u>, has no inheritance in the kingdom of Christ and God.*

1 Corinthians 5:11 (ESV) But now I am writing to you not to associate with anyone who bears the name of brother if he is guilty of sexual immorality or greed, or is an idolater, <u>reviler,</u> drunkard, or swindler—not even to eat with such a one.

In 1 Corinthians 5:11, the designation "Or a railer" is essentially translated as "reviler," pointing to an individual characterized by the use of harsh, coarse, and bitter language. This person habitually engages in verbally abusing others, either through spoken or written expressions that are disparaging and abusive. Such an individual demonstrates a lack of concern for the feelings of others, and this behavior starkly contradicts the spirit of Christianity and the exemplary conduct set by the Master. The fruits of the Holy Spirit, which include love, kindness, and gentleness, completely contrast this rude and abrasive demeanor.

1 Corinthians 5:11 (ESV) But now I am writing to you not to associate with anyone who bears the name of brother if he is guilty of sexual immorality or greed, or is an idolater, reviler, <u>drunkard,</u> or swindler—not even to eat with such a one.

The inclusion of "Or a drunkard" may seem unusual as a criterion for identifying a church member. However, in dealing with real issues in some churches, the apostle addresses the severity of this matter. In my pastoral experiences involving individuals struggling with severe drinking problems, the issue of judgment often arises. It is never right to do the wrong thing. Church leadership frequently does the wrong thing for fear of offending family members.

The bottom line is this.
Come Out From Among Them

Chapter 13

Do Not Associate With Unruly Christians
1 Corinthians 5:11
Part 6

The apostle's guidance in 1 Corinthians chapter 5 becomes a scriptural foundation for addressing such concerns. Some individuals within the Corinthian church, akin to situations in contemporary congregations, were trapped by the destructive grip of alcohol addiction. The apostle unequivocally advises Christians to refrain from fellowship with such individuals, recognizing this vice's profound and historical impact on the church.

The following statement saddens me. Surprisingly, there is often less peril in associating with openly lost worldly individuals than with immature and carnal Christians. The Corinthian church, while not overtly falling into open idolatry, made compromises by allowing church members to engage in open sins, including participating in eating things offered to idols, indicating a level of concession to heathen practices.

1 Corinthians 5:11 (ESV) But now I am writing to you not to associate with anyone who bears the name of brother if he is guilty of sexual immorality or greed, or is an idolater, reviler, drunkard, or swindler—<u>not even to eat with such a one.</u>

Come Out From Among Them

The apostle clarifies that his prohibition against keeping company with individuals of the worldly character mentioned above pertains to those identified as Christian brothers. These individuals had undergone scrutiny, professing their faith and being received into the church.

However, they were later discovered guilty of gross and unrepentant sins. This behavior revealed the necessity of the apostle's guidance to separate those who persist in such transgressions from those within the Christian community. In 1 Corinthians 5:11, the Apostle Paul gives the proper Biblical course of action to which one must adhere. This action of separating ourselves from them does not mean we do not love those participating in these sins. It means that we love God and the commands in His Word more. Loving someone does not dictate that we must walk in unity with them.

Let's delve into the concept of "Come out from among them" and the instructions given by Paul regarding the association with individuals who profess to be Christian brothers but engage in immoral conduct. Paul emphasizes the importance of avoiding fellowship with those who are notorious for their involvement in sins such as fornication, covetousness, idolatry, extortion, railing, and drunkenness.

According to Paul, if such individuals persist in unrepentant and incorrigible behavior even after receiving a warning, the church must remove them from communion and distance themselves from sharing meals with them. This separation denies them civil conversation and familiarity, as the church is instructed to "come out from among them."

The rationale behind this action is twofold. Firstly, it aims to vindicate the honor of the church's faith in a holy God. Secondly, it seeks to prevent the stumbling of the weak within the congregation. From the perspective of the offenders, the intent is to induce shame and prompt repentance through the church's withdrawal of fellowship.

Paul goes so far as to command that Christians should not even eat with such individuals. In the cultural context of that time and in many cultures today, sharing a meal symbolizes friendship and partnership. Paul stresses the gravity of the issue by advising the Corinthian Christians against continuing fellowship with a professed Christian who persists in unrepentant sinful behavior.

He communicates that this separation is not just a physical act but a spiritual one, as it signifies a disassociation from any form of contact or fellowship with the offender. The goal is to refrain from actions that might acknowledge the individual as a brother and to avoid sharing the same table. A parallel instruction is echoed by the apostle John in 2 John 1:10-11, emphasizing the seriousness of maintaining distance from those who propagate a false gospel.

> *2 John 1:10-11 (ESV) If anyone comes to you and does not bring this teaching, do not receive him into your house or give him any greeting, 11 for whoever greets him takes part in his wicked works.*

In 1 Corinthians 5, the central message is a call for true Christians to completely disown Christian individuals who are continually engaged in sinful behavior and are unrepentant. I know this flies in the face with our concept of what Biblical unity is. Don't get upset at the messenger. The message came from God to the church as a warning and for our protection. Again, this does not mean we do not love the person. Remember that this action comes after repeated attempts to get the individuals to confess their sins and repent.

Paul instructs believers not to engage in any actions that might imply recognition of such individuals as Christian brothers. The essence of this message can be summarized as urging these individuals to demonstrate their professed faith through their actions – essentially challenging them to let their walk validate their talk.

This perspective reflects a stance beyond merely accepting someone's testimony of being a Christian. The emphasis is on evaluating the authenticity of one's faith based on one's fruits rather than relying solely on one's profession. In line with Christ's teaching that we will recognize true believers by their fruits, the message stresses the importance of tangible evidence of a genuine and transformed Christian life.

Notably, the severity of the rule, as articulated in Corinthians, regarding the expulsion of a professing Christian from the church and the refusal to share meals with them is highlighted. The standards are more stringent for those who claim to be Christians compared to those who openly acknowledge themselves as spiritually lost pagans. The underlying principle is to reinforce the idea that actions speak louder than words, particularly within the context of Christian fellowship.

To further elaborate on this concept, let's consider Peter's perspective on a believer who returns to the sins of the world. Okay, I am about to give one of my favorite sayings when I am about to drop a heavy Scripture that challenges mainline denominational teachings. It is time to put your "big boy" pants on. Additional insight from Peter's teachings can provide a broader understanding of the consequences and considerations when a believer turns away from their faith and reverts to a lifestyle contrary to Christian principles. That is a kind way of saying they have walked away from God and the faith.

> *2 Peter 2:21-22 (ESV) For it would have been better for them never to have known the way of righteousness than after knowing it to turn back from the holy commandment delivered to them. 22 What the true proverb says has happened to them: "The dog returns to its own vomit, and the sow, after washing herself, returns to wallow in the mire."*

The apparent toughness of the judgment in 1 Corinthians 5 regarding the expulsion of individuals engaged in sinful behavior, particularly those professing to be Christians, can be attributed to a twofold necessity. Firstly, there is a compelling need to maintain the purity of the church. The strict measures are in place to safeguard the sanctity and moral integrity of the Christian community, ensuring that it remains untainted by the influence of persistent sin within its ranks.

Secondly, the severity of the judgment also serves the purpose of avoiding any semblance that Christians are patrons or friends of the wicked world. The intention is to prevent the church from conveying the impression that it condones or associates with unrepentant sinners, thereby upholding a clear distinction between the values of the Christian community and those of the secular world. The shadow of this separation of God's people from the lost is seen throughout the Old Testament, which commands that Israel was not to walk in the ways of those outside their faith.

Essentially, the church is cautioned against creating an impression that all who enter its doors are automatically regarded as brothers in the faith. The imperative here is to maintain a discerning approach, ensuring that a transformed life and adherence to Christian principles substantiate the identity of a genuine Christian. The strict measures stress the commitment to preserving the church as a holy and distinct entity, free from the compromising influence of the world.

In the context of individuals who professed to be Christians but were immersed in the vices of drunkenness and lascivious behavior, there was a concern that Paul's acceptance of them might inadvertently convey compromise of God's command to be holy as He is holy. The necessity for complete separation and withdrawal from all forms of communion in those times was driven by the imperative to shield the church from damaging reports circulating throughout the Christian world, akin to the challenges posed by mass media in our contemporary era.

The fear was that the association with individuals engaging in such sinful conduct could potentially tarnish the reputation of the entire church and its spiritual leaders. In a manner reminiscent of today's media landscape, where negative perceptions of a few individuals can cast a shadow over a whole group, the church sought to protect itself from damaging reports. One bad apple in the group could brand the entire church as being sinful and wicked. Throughout history, Christians faced accusations from pagans, ranging from crimes to abominations, and these reports posed significant threats to the credibility and integrity of the church.

Paul's guidance emphasized the need to draw an unequivocal line of separation. The objective was to ensure that the actions of individuals engaging in sinful behavior did not compromise the collective reputation of the Christian community. If the church's reputation was tarnished, so was the testimony of God and His commands to "come out from among them." Remember the question of the women of the city to the Shulamite woman in the Song of Solomon? The book of the Song of Solomon is a picture of Christ to the church. Therefore, the question would be from the spiritually lost of the world to the church concerning Christ,

> *Song of Solomon 5:9 (ESV) Others What is your beloved more than another beloved, O most beautiful among women? What is your beloved more than another beloved, that you thus adjure us?*

Today, the world asks the church, "What makes your God any different from any other God?" This question is driven by the poor example of the church in separating herself from the world.

Paul explained this directive of separation by acknowledging that, despite the imperative for total separation within the church, there were still opportunities for acts of kindness and compassion toward neighbors, relatives, and those in distress or need.

This recognition implies that while maintaining a strict boundary within the church is essential for preserving its moral and righteous standing, there is room for extending love, empathy, and support to those outside the church who may be facing challenges or difficulties.

The call for separation is not an absolute prohibition on displaying love, kindness, and compassion but rather a strategic measure to safeguard the church's integrity while allowing for compassionate outreach to those beyond its immediate boundaries. Paul expressed the limitations of evaluating a person's moral lifestyle to those within the Christian faith community. But we cannot preach the righteousness of Christ and the changed life if we continue to allow unconfessed and unrepentant sin in the camp. Paul said in 1 Corinthians 5:12 that he (or us) had no authority to judge or assess those outside the Christian faith.

The bottom line is this.
Come Out From Among Them

Chapter 14

Do Not Associate With Unruly Christians
1 Corinthians 5:12
Part 7

1 Corinthians 5:12 (ESV) <u>For what have I to do with judging outsiders?</u> Is it not those inside the church whom you are to judge?

In his communication with the Corinthian church, Paul explicitly conveyed that his role did not involve passing judgment on individuals outside the church community. He emphasized that those beyond the church's boundaries were beyond his governmental authority and not a matter of his concern, except they become born again. Again, we must understand that Paul clarified that his focus was not directed toward the spiritually lost or unbelievers, commonly called "those outside the Church." This substantiates that those Paul addressed in 1 Corinthians who were guilty of unrepentant sins were Christians.

It's crucial to clarify that Paul's stance on not judging those outside the church did not imply indifference towards their salvation and eternal destiny. Instead, his emphasis was on addressing their sinful lifestyle. Paul recognized that sinners knew how to sin, and even if they managed to adopt a more moral lifestyle and minimize their immoral actions, they remained lost and were classified as children of darkness.

Come Out From Among Them

Paul's discernment went beyond merely identifying the external manifestations of sin; he understood that the fundamental issue with those outside the church was not solely their sinful behavior but their spiritual state of being lost and without Christ. In highlighting this distinction, Paul focused on the core issue of salvation and their need for a relationship with Christ, which exceeded the surface-level focus on sinful actions. Sometimes, we spend more time and energy seeking to get the lost world to increase their moral standards then getting them to receive Christ for their eternal redemption.

The essence of Paul's message to the Corinthian church was a declaration of his lack of authority over the spiritually lost. He asserted that he held no jurisdiction over their conduct and behavior. His rules and directives, he made clear, applied exclusively to those within the church – those who professed knowledge of the Lord Jesus Christ.

The term "judge," used by Paul, is the Greek word "krino," which has various meanings such as deciding judicially, condemning, punishing, damning, decreeing, questioning, pronouncing opinions on right and wrong, summoning to trial, ruling, and governing. Paul underscored that, as a Christian apostle, he did not possess this jurisdiction over those outside the church.

Outsiders, as defined by Paul, were individuals beyond the church community, characterized as pagans, people of the world, those who had rejected Christ, children of wrath, and children of darkness. Paul emphasized to the Corinthian church that he had no authority to admonish, reprove, censure, or condemn those outside the church for their ungodly behavior. The scope of ecclesiastical jurisdiction did not extend to the actions and authority of those outside Christ.

Paul addressed a common trend among Christians – the tendency to judge those outside the church, a role reserved for God alone. He highlighted the neglect of maintaining purity within the church, particularly in the realm of politics. Paul observed that many believers were quick to pass judgment on politicians, mistakenly viewing them as saviors of the world, thereby diverting attention from the imperative of preserving purity within the church.

The bottom line is this.

Come Out From Among Them

Chapter 15

Do Not Associate With Unruly Christians
1 Corinthians 5:12
Part 8

1 Corinthians 5:12 (ESV) For what have I to do with judging outsiders? <u>Is it not those inside the church whom you are to judge?</u>

The phrase "You are not supposed to judge" is a common assertion, often vocalized by individuals unfamiliar with the teachings found in God's Word regarding this matter. In essence, Paul's message underscores the notion that engaging in judgment (evaluation or assessment) within the church community is expected and required. In other words, we are responsible for judging (evaluating) our Christian brothers and sisters in the Lord in their spiritual walk.

Galatians 6:1 (ESV) Brothers, if anyone is caught in any transgression, you who are spiritual should restore him in a spirit of gentleness. Keep watch on yourself, lest you too be tempted.

The essence of Paul's perspective is captured in the idea that the judgment process initiates from within the house of God. "Judgment begins in the house of God."

1 Peter 4:17 (ESV) For it is time for judgment to begin at the household of God; and if it begins with us, what will be the outcome for those who do not obey the gospel of God?

By emphasizing the responsibility of evaluating and addressing matters within the church, Paul highlights the significance of focusing on the internal dynamics and relationships within the Christian community. The bottom line is we are to prioritize self-examination and accountability within the context of the church rather than extending judgment to those outside the body of Christ. Sinners know how to sin. Believers must learn how to live holy and sanctified lives.

1 Corinthians 5:12 (ESV) For what have I to do with _judging_ outsiders? Is it not those inside the church whom you are to _judge_?

In the context of 1 Corinthians 5:12, the apostle Paul employed the Greek word "krino" to convey the concept of judgment. Notably, he used the same term when addressing the act of judging individuals within the church community as he did when expressing his stance on refraining from passing judgment on those outside the church or the spiritually lost. This linguistic consistency stresses Paul's deliberate choice of terminology, emphasizing the uniformity in his perspective on judgment.

The term "judge" means deciding judicially, condemning, punishing, damning, decreeing, questioning, pronouncing opinions on right and wrong, summoning to trial, ruling, and governing.

When we make the false claim that we lack the authority to judge fellow Christians, it reflects a deficiency in our spiritual understanding of this matter. It signifies a failure to grasp our significant responsibility towards one another within the Christian community and, importantly, towards our heavenly Father. Understanding and acknowledging this responsibility is crucial for the sanctity and purity of the church.

This recognition is integral to how Jesus envisions presenting the church to Himself—a holy and untarnished people devoid of any spot or blemish. We don't mind being a "forgiven" people. We speak often about how the Father has forgiven us over and over ten thousand times. Our issue comes with being a "holy and sanctified" people. Many in the church community sincerely proclaim, "We are not supposed to judge." They may think they sound spiritual by echoing this false man-made statement. It is an attempt to take one verse in Matthew and use it like a banner in protest. Again, these folks would rather live in the state of continually being forgiven for their sins than come to a place of being challenged and gaining victory over their sins.

Our willingness to pass judgment or evaluate our brother's Christian walk within the Christian community contributes to realizing this vision of a pure and holy church before the Lord. It emphasizes the importance of fostering a fellowship of mutual support, accountability, and spiritual growth, aligning with the divine standard set forth by our heavenly Father and exemplified by the teachings of Jesus.

> *Ephesians 5:26-27 (ESV) that he might sanctify her, having cleansed her by the washing of water with the word, 27 so that he might present the church to himself in splendor, without spot or wrinkle or any*

such thing, that she might be holy and without blemish.

In the context of 1 Corinthians 5, Paul conveys a clear message regarding the authority and responsibility of judging those within the church. He stresses that if the members are to engage in the act of judgment (evaluation and assessment) within the Christian community, they also bear the authority and responsibility to implement discipline and administer punishment to individuals involved in unrepentant sexual sins.

Through the inspiration of the Holy Spirit, the Apostle employs a rhetorical strategy to spur the Corinthian church members into action by posing questions that prompt self-examination. He asks, "Do not you judge those that are within?" Essentially, he urges them to recognize their authority and responsibility to exercise judgment over their community. It is like saying, "You do judge (evaluate) those in your church, right?"

The Apostle Paul goes further, expressing that it would have been commendable if they had utilized their power to admonish and reprove those who had continually committed these sins. Again. The issue was not just that someone sinned because we all are guilty of that. Paul addressed those who continued to sin and refused to confess or repent. The rhetorical question, "Do you not judge those who are inside?" is a call to action, imploring them to take decisive steps. He emphasizes the need to remove, through disciplinary measures, the unrepentant sinful Christian from their midst.

Paul contends that the Corinthian Christians were falling short of their duty to pass judgment (evaluation and assessment) where it was warranted. He admonishes them for overlooking the unrepentant sinner among them, cautioning against turning a blind eye to such transgressions in the misguided belief that their neglect constitutes a form of Christian love. Paul urges a recalibration of their approach, emphasizing the importance of exercising judgment where necessary and maintaining purity and integrity in the Christian community. In 1 Corinthians 5:13, Paul informed believers that only God judges the spiritually lost, those outside the faith.

The bottom line is this.

Come Out From Among Them

Chapter 16

Do Not Associate With Unruly Christians
1 Corinthians 5:13
Part 9

> **1 Corinthians 5:13 (ESV)** <u>**God judges those outside.**</u> **"Purge the evil person from among you."**

Consider those who are outside the church as individuals who, in a spiritual sense, exist as heathens dwelling in the fallen worldly system and darkness. Their judgment ultimately rests with God.

Individuals not affiliated with the church fall directly under God's distinct government and judgment rather than the church. Our responsibility towards them is rooted in love, and we are tasked with conveying the message of the gospel to them through both our words and actions. Those of us who have found salvation in our Lord Jesus Christ are identified as saints, acknowledging that we, too, still grapple with sin. In contrast, those outside the church—those who are lost—are categorized as sinners and find themselves under the judgment of God. Their guilt and punishment have already been established. Unless they repent, confess Christ as Savior, and are justified through the redemptive work of our Lord Jesus Christ, they will die in their sins.

> *John 3:18-20 (ESV) Whoever believes in him is not condemned, but whoever does not believe is condemned already, because he has not believed in*

> the name of the only Son of God. 19 And this is the judgment: the light has come into the world, and people loved the darkness rather than the light because their works were evil. 20 For everyone who does wicked things hates the light and does not come to the light, lest his works should be exposed.

While those beyond the church may not be subject to correction or punishment by the apostle or a congregation affiliated with our Lord Jesus Christ, it is imperative to recognize that they will not escape consequences for their sins and immoral conduct. Divine justice awaits them as God, the ultimate authority over heaven and earth, will hold them accountable for their sins, such as fornication, covetousness, idolatry, extortion, and more. Those who choose to live under the law will be judged by the law, and if they break one law, they are guilty of all.

The God who governs the heavens and the earth will serve as the ultimate arbiter, passing judgment and condemning them based on rejection of Jesus Christ as Savior as recorded in the Scriptures. The Book of Books will declare the words, deeds, and thoughts of those who refused to accept Christ and His work on the cross.

> Revelation 20:11-13 (ESV) Then I saw a great white throne and him who was seated on it. From his presence earth and sky fled away, and no place was found for them. 12 And I saw the dead, great and small, standing before the throne, and books were opened. Then another book was opened, which is the book of life. And the dead were judged by what was written in the books, according to what they had done. 13 And the sea gave up the dead who were in it,

> *Death and Hades gave up the dead who were in them, and they were judged, each one of them, according to what they had done.*

1 Corinthians 5:13 (ESV) God judges those outside. "Purge the evil person from among you."

The phrase "Purge the evil person from among you" in 1 Corinthians 5:13 resonates as a call for excommunication, indicating the imperative to distance or expel an individual from the community of believers. This action represents the church's authority given by the Father over its members, embodying the responsibility to exercise judgment (evaluation). It is a solemn duty mandated upon the church to pass this judgment on individuals who have openly transgressed against the Word and character of God the Father and our Lord Jesus Christ while refusing to confess and repent of their sins.

In our modern-day contemporary church practices, rather than executing the removal of the unrepentant and wicked individual from the community, there is a tendency to conceal, hide, or turn a blind eye to the wrongful deeds committed. This departure from the original intention of purging the evil person reflects a shift in approach within some modern churches so as not to "offend" anyone. Many churches make great efforts to conceal the wrongdoer's actions rather than address the issue at its core.

> *Matthew 18:16-17 (ESV) But if he does not listen, take one or two others along with you, that every charge may be established by the evidence of two or three witnesses. 17 If he refuses to listen to them, tell it to the church. And if he refuses to listen even to the*

church, let him be to you as a Gentile and a tax collector.

In undertaking this course of action, our sincere hope is that our intentions are not misconstrued and that we are not unfairly perceived as cold-hearted or lacking in love. It's crucial to understand that this decision is not a humanly devised strategy. Rather, it aligns with the divine framework established by the Father for the proper functioning of the church. The Creator's guidelines dictate how the redeemed should navigate their journey in corporate fellowship with Him and one another.

The repercussions of failed discipline and a lack of accountability are evident globally, manifesting in households and the church community. The prevalence of these issues in Christian homes and churches stresses the importance of adhering to the principles laid out by God for the functioning of the church.

I feel it is essential for us to recall God's reasoning for excluding an unrepentant believer from the fellowship of saints. This reasoning, grounded in the Father's divine wisdom, serves as a guiding principle for maintaining the sanctity and integrity of the community of the redeemed.

The foundational understanding is that as believers, we are called holy and set apart for the Lord. This sanctification necessitates separation from those who are not aligned with these principles. The command to be separate implies abstaining from intimate association with the lost and Christians walking in continual unrepentant sins.

Maintaining this separation is not solely for the preservation of one's own character but also to prevent corruption by ungodly examples of non-believers and Christians who are backslidden. It is a precaution against being led astray by their conduct, which may potentially lead to neglecting vital spiritual disciplines such as prayer and participation in true fellowship with other saints.

Therefore, the rationale behind this action of casting the unrepentant Christian from us is twofold. First, it aims to vindicate the honor of the church's faith in a holy God. We are to be holy as He is holy. Secondly, it seeks to prevent the stumbling of the weak within the congregation.

From the perspective of the offenders, the intent is to induce shame and prompt repentance through the church's withdrawal of fellowship. The withdrawal of fellowship by the church is a deliberate measure designed to communicate the seriousness of the actions committed. It serves as a means to prompt self-examination and a behavior change, emphasizing the significance of aligning with the principles upheld by God's Word.

The bottom line is this.

Come Out From Among Them

Chapter 17

Withdraw From Those That Teach Unsound Doctrine
1 Timothy 6:3-5
Part 1

We must be resolute in distancing ourselves from individuals who engage in the sinful behaviors detailed in 1 Timothy 6:3-5. It is imperative to clarify that this separation pertains not to isolated instances of wrongdoing but to a persistent pattern of living in these transgressions without repentance. Recalling the warning in the Scriptures is crucial, as it emphasizes that consistent association with corrupt individuals can corrupt one's own moral compass. Therefore, we are called not only to avoid the influence of those entrenched in continual sinful conduct but also to guard our integrity by maintaining distance from such associations.

> *1 Timothy 6:3-5 (ESV) If anyone teaches a different doctrine and does not agree with the sound words of our Lord Jesus Christ and the teaching that accords with godliness, 4 he is puffed up with conceit and understands nothing. He has an unhealthy craving for controversy and for quarrels about words, which produce envy, dissension, slander, evil suspicions, 5 and constant friction among people who are depraved in mind and deprived of the truth, imagining that godliness is a means of gain.*

1 Corinthians 15:33 (ESV) Do not be deceived: "Bad company ruins good morals."

Look at the last line of 1 Timothy 6:5 in the KJV.

*1 Timothy 6:5 (KJV) Perverse disputings of men of corrupt minds, and destitute of the truth, supposing that gain is godliness: **from such withdraw thyself**.*

To comprehend the message conveyed in 1 Timothy 6:3-5, dissecting the passage into smaller segments is beneficial. In these verses, the apostle Paul's instructions to the church are insightful and instructive, urging believers to exercise discernment and wisdom in their interactions and associations.

Maintaining Sound Doctrine Over Emotions

In 1 Timothy 6:3-5, Paul begins by addressing the importance of sound doctrine and avoiding false teachings. To avoid false teachings, one must avoid false teachers. He emphasizes the significance of adhering to the teachings of Christ and the apostles, stressing that deviating from these foundational truths can lead to a spiritual detriment.

In the 1 Timothy 6 passage, Paul highlights the character of those who propagate false doctrines. He describes them as individuals who are conceited and lack understanding, demonstrating a propensity for contentious arguments and disputes. Their motives are driven by a desire for personal gain rather than genuine concern for the well-being of others or the truth of the Gospel.

Paul emphasizes the necessity for believers to reject their teachings and distance themselves from such individuals and their false ways. He cautions against being swayed or misled by eloquent rhetoric or persuasive arguments devoid of truth and genuine spiritual insight. Too much Bible teaching today seems to imply a lot while saying nothing.

Furthermore, Paul warns that embracing false teachings and aligning oneself with those who promote them can lead to spiritual ruin and moral compromise. He urges believers to uphold the integrity of their faith and to remain steadfast in the truth of God's Word. Believers are to resist the allure of false doctrines and the influence of those who propagate them.

In essence, Paul's instructions in 1 Timothy 6:3-5 serve as a warning to exercise discernment, vigilance, and steadfastness in the face of doctrinal challenges and false teachings. He implores believers to prioritize sound doctrine, reject falsehoods, and maintain a firm commitment to the truth of the Gospel, safeguarding both their spiritual well-being and the integrity of the Church as a whole. The deity and blood atonement of our Lord Jesus Christ are under attack. The attack is within the walls of our institutionalized organizations called "church."

The bottom line is this.

Come Out From Among Them

Chapter 18

Withdraw From Those That Teach Unsound Doctrine
1 Timothy 6:3
Part 2

1 Timothy 6:3 (ESV) <u>If anyone teaches a different doctrine</u> and does not agree with the sound words of our Lord Jesus Christ and the teaching that accords with godliness,

We will start by breaking 1 Timothy 6:3 down word by word to see what the Father is telling us and ways we are to obey to maintain integrity in the fellowship of believers. In the early church, the propagation of false doctrines was considered grave, evoking serious concern among believers. However, contemporary attitudes toward doctrinal integrity appear to have shifted.

What has happened to us? First, the church as a whole has an unbiblical view of what Christian unity is. Secondly, the church loves its superstars and heroes. The more famous or financially successful someone in Hollywood or on TV becomes, the more the church makes every effort to canonize them into the Christian faith. They can hold and practice demonic doctrines and believe in universalism, but once they use the name "god" in one of their conversations, the church soars through social media that this person is a spiritual giant in the faith.

Come Out From Among Them

There's a troubling trend wherein a misguided notion of unity prevails, fostering an environment where almost anything is tolerated within the church as long as it doesn't offend. Alongside this, a misinterpretation of Biblical teachings on judgment has taken root, leading many to believe they are forbidden from discerning right from wrong. Therefore, everyone can believe whatever is right in their own eyes.

As we delve deeper into Paul's first letter to Timothy, we encounter a recurring theme that stresses the imperative for vigilance against the misuse of God's Word. Paul reiterates the need for Timothy to remain discerning, especially in the face of those who distort or misinterpret Scripture for their own agendas.

The apostle's warnings serve as a sober reminder of the dangers inherent in neglecting doctrinal purity and giving in to the pressures of false unity and indiscriminate acceptance. In embracing such ideologies, the foundational principles of Biblical truth and discernment are compromised, giving rise to a climate where individual interpretations and personal convictions supersede the authority and intent of Scripture.

Paul's exhortations to Timothy resonate with contemporary believers, urging us to uphold God's Word and guard against the subtle encroachments of false teachings and misinterpretations. By remaining steadfast in our commitment to sound doctrine and Biblical truth, we uphold the integrity of the faith and preserve the purity of the Gospel message for generations to come.

1 Timothy 1:3-7 (ESV) As I urged you when I was going to Macedonia, remain at Ephesus so that you may charge certain persons not to teach any different doctrine, 4 nor to devote themselves to myths and endless genealogies, which promote speculations rather than the stewardship from God that is by faith. 5 The aim of our charge is love that issues from a pure heart and a good conscience and a sincere faith. 6 Certain persons, by swerving from these, have wandered away into vain discussion, 7 desiring to be teachers of the law, without understanding either what they are saying or the things about which they make confident assertions.

Within the context of 1 Timothy 6:3-5, there exists a significant danger of replacing the clear and straightforward teachings of God's Word with an undue emphasis on prophecies, visions, and other supposedly supernatural experiences. Although we embrace supernatural gifts for today, we do so only if manifested by the Holy Spirit and aligned with the Word and character of God. In his counsel to Timothy, Paul stresses the gravity of the dangerous trend of false doctrine.

The risk lies in deviating from the solid foundation of Biblical truth. Deviating from truth causes one to become trapped by the allure of fleshly and sensational spiritual encounters that are not manifestations by the anointing of the Holy Spirit. By prioritizing mystical experiences over the timeless wisdom contained in Scripture, believers open themselves to deception and distortion of the Gospel message. The essence lies in the relationship between the letter of the Law and the guiding influence of the Spirit. It is not prioritizing one over the other but recognizing the indispensable synergy that occurs when the Word and the Spirit operate in harmony.

> *2 Corinthians 3:4-9 (ESV) Such is the confidence that we have through Christ toward God. 5 Not that we are sufficient in ourselves to claim anything as coming from us, but our sufficiency is from God, 6 who has made us sufficient to be ministers of a new covenant, not of the letter but of the Spirit. For the letter kills, but the Spirit gives life. 7 Now if the ministry of death, carved in letters on stone, came with such glory that the Israelites could not gaze at Moses' face because of its glory, which was being brought to an end, 8 will not the ministry of the Spirit have even more glory? 9 For if there was glory in the ministry of condemnation, the ministry of righteousness must far exceed it in glory.*

The letter of the Law provides the foundational principles and precepts that govern our understanding of God's will and His standards of righteousness. It serves as a roadmap for ethical living and spiritual growth, offering clear guidance on conducting ourselves according to divine truth.

However, mere adherence to the letter of the Law, devoid of the redemptive power and guidance of the Holy Spirit, can lead to legalism and spiritual death. The Spirit breathes life into the written Word, illuminating its meaning and empowering believers to apply its principles daily.

The Word and the Spirit are inseparable partners in the Christian journey, working in tandem to convict hearts, inspire obedience, and impart wisdom. When the Holy Spirit reveals the Word to us, it becomes a dynamic force for renewal and transformation, guiding believers into deeper intimacy with God and conformity to His likeness.

The Person of the Holy Spirit operates within the framework of God's revealed truth, ensuring that His guidance aligns with the principles and teachings of Scripture. Through the Word, we discern the authenticity of spiritual experiences. The promptings of the Holy Spirit safeguard against deception and error from following emotionalism and sensationalism over God's Word.

The dynamic working between the Word and the Spirit is essential for vibrant faith and authentic discipleship. It is a harmonious integration of God's revealed truth and His empowering presence, leading believers into a deeper and more intimate relationship with their Creator.

Paul's admonition to Timothy serves as a vital reminder of the importance of discernment and steadfast adherence to the teachings of Scripture. It stresses the need to maintain a balanced perspective, recognizing the value of spiritual gifts and experiences while anchoring them firmly in the unchanging truths of God's Word.

Paul's warning calls believers to exercise wisdom and discernment, ensuring their faith remains grounded in the authoritative revelation of God's Word. Grounded in the Word will guard against being swayed by the subjective nature of supernatural encounters or famous personalities filled with charity and charisma. We must maintain the attitude of exalting our Lord Jesus Christ in all we do. Let's continue with 1 Timothy 6:3

The bottom line is this.
Come Out From Among Them

Chapter 19

Withdraw From Those That Teach Unsound Doctrine
1 Timothy 6:3
Part 3

1 Timothy 6:3 (ESV) If anyone teaches a different doctrine <u>and does not agree with the sound words of our Lord Jesus Christ and the teaching that accords with godliness,</u>

The words of our Lord Jesus Christ are the doctrines that He taught and preached when He was on earth. The doctrines relating to Christ written by others concerning His humanity, deity, offices, grace, righteousness, sacrifice, and resurrection make up our belief system. These doctrines relate to what He is, has done, does, and will do.

Paul warned Timothy against those who bring argumentative rhetoric and those who have left the Word of God to promote their own ideas with the doctrines of man and demons. He warned Timothy against those who seemed to treat the Word of God more as a plaything instead of as a precious gift.

This instruction reveals that one does not have to be an active opponent of God's Word to be an enemy of it. We oppose God's Word if we fail to give the Bible its rightful place in our lives and our preaching. I was shocked to read that only 20% of Christians accept the Bible as the literal Word of God.

For those who love the Lord Jesus Christ, leaving the teachings and words of our Christ might seem like an unnecessary warning. Yet, the apostle Paul felt the warning was necessary because those who misuse God's truth don't advertise themselves that way. A false teacher doesn't introduce himself as such. They often come as wolves in sheep's clothing and claim to honor God's Word while misusing it. There are different ways that some people reject the truth of God's Word.

- *Some boldly deny God's Word as such.*
- *Some ignore God's Word, bypassing the Scriptures they don't like.*
- *Some explain away God's Word with their manmade traditions and doctrines.*
- *Some twist God's Word, using it as a toy to be played with in debates and disputes. Pulling the Scriptures out of context, they attempt to make it say what it does not mean within the whole context.*

Some Christians can be surrounded by God's truth and not have it affect their lives. Curiosity or interest in God's Word without submission to it is a grave danger.

The time is upon us when we are overwhelmed with useless information. No matter what we want to believe, we can find someone on social media who will teach what we like to hear and twist the Scriptures to an attempt to prove their point.

It is easy to regard the Bible as useless information or as only one source of information among millions of answers. The Bible is no longer viewed as *"The sole authority and source"* of information for humanity needed to deal with sin and the teachings for spiritual growth. It is no longer viewed as the Book with the necessary truth that confronts and transforms our lives.

Listen! Bible study is not meant to be a trivial pursuit where we treat God's Word as a book of useless information. The Bible was not meant to be a sourcebook for answering board game questions. The Bible was never to be treated as a history book that lacked the authority and right to change lives.

The bottom line is this.
Come Out From Among Them

Chapter 20

Withdraw From Those That Teach Unsound Doctrine
1 Timothy 6:3
Part 4

1 Timothy 6:3 (ESV) If anyone teaches a different doctrine and does not agree with the <u>sound words</u> of our Lord Jesus Christ and <u>the teaching that accords with godliness</u>,

Paul warns young Timothy in 1 Timothy 6:3 that they will not agree with the sound words of our Lord Jesus Christ and teachings that lead us to godliness. The statement "sound words" is the same as wholesome words. Let's look at the danger behind the urgency of Paul's warning.

The opposite of wholesome in our everyday speech is that which *tends to produce disease,* but the opposite of the Greek term "sound words" is *that which is already unsound or diseased.*

The apostle's thought is that there is nothing unhealthy about the words of Jesus. The words of the Lord are healthy and wholesome so that all who believe and obey them become stronger, nobler, and sounder in all the qualities of Christian maturity. The opposite is also true. Those who reject the Word are already diseased. Now, let us see how this statement of Paul may be verified and illustrated.

The fruit reveals the root. The whole Gospel message is the mystery of godliness. It is verified when we see people who are supernaturally born again immediately tend to promote true godliness in word, deed, and thought.

The holiness of the heart is personal evidence to the believers that they have experienced true salvation. The holiness of life is evidence of a changed life and a changed attitude toward the world. The covenant of God's grace provides for both internal and external holiness. In this, we see true Christians making the right choices when opting for God's Word over the pleasures of the world.

As much as I love to teach and instruct in the Word of truth, it fills my heart with joy to see a believer make the right choice to follow God and His ways from their study of the Word, personal conviction, and spiritual maturity.

Nothing seems so tiring than constantly re-educating someone because of his immaturity, weakness, and helplessness. I don't want to be required to follow a Christian around each day to tell him precisely what he must do in every emergency or crisis. I don't want a believer to grow dependent on my presence and counsel and never be able to stand on his own. The apostle Paul says in Ephesians, "Having done all else, stand." Within the leadership and guidance of the Holy Spirit, we all are to learn to make godly choices and stand firm on God's truth. If someone always needs to be watched to do the right thing, he can never be depended upon or trusted.

> **1 Timothy 6:3 (ESV) If anyone teaches a different doctrine and does not agree with <u>the sound words of our Lord Jesus Christ and the teaching that accords with godliness</u>,**

In 1 Timothy, the Apostle Paul reminded us to take all our teachings back to the teachings of Christ. The teachings of the Sermon on the Mount prove the practicality of the gospel in the demonstrations our Lord gave. Our Lord Jesus Christ said a candle was not lit to be looked at or talked about, but it might give light to all in the house. In other words, the Christian faith and life should be used rather than discussed. It is meant to illuminate all the obscurities of life's pathway to help keep man walking in the straight and narrow.

Our Lord's teaching increased godliness in conversation and actions in others. The doctrine of godliness means the teaching which makes men more like the character of God. This character in us is manifested in our walking in His holiness, righteousness, forgiveness, grace, and love.

But in sharp contrast with this lifestyle of godliness, Paul presented the unwholesomeness or unhealthiness of those with an ungodly lifestyle within the church. The effects of this were visible in the character of those who accepted and taught it, as seen in 1 Timothy 6:4-5.

The bottom line is this.

Come Out From Among Them

Chapter 21

Withdraw From Those That Teach Unsound Doctrine
1 Timothy 6:4
Part 5

*1 Timothy 6:4 (ESV) <u>**he is puffed up with conceit and understands nothing.**</u> **He has an unhealthy craving for controversy and for quarrels about words, which produce envy, dissension, slander, evil suspicions,***

He is proud. This phrase means that he is lifted up with his fancied superior knowledge of the nature and organization of religion. The Greek verb means to smoke, fume, and then to be inflated. The unhealthy state of ungodly people is seen in their self-sufficiency. The apostle Paul says they are proud or puffed up and carried away with conceit, knowing nothing.

Paul describes those who misuse God's Word for their own gain. Yet, they don't see or admit their lack of spiritual knowledge. Unfortunately, they can convince immature believers that they are experts in God's truth when all along they misuse it. These unhealthy and ungodly people have formulas and elaborate schemes laid out for their complicated false doctrines. Still, they will not allow the simplicity of God's Word to speak for itself. They are always trying to put their spin on their doctrines as modern politicians do. They say a lot that means nothing. This is the worst kind of pride. It shows a group of people related to the church who have more confidence in their worldly intellect, wisdom, and opinions than in the straightforward truth coming from God's Word.

Pride could make preachers think their stories, opinions, or humor could be more important than the clear teaching from the Word of God. Paul said this type of person may be filled with facts and stories, but they don't know anything substantial. They know nothing of the true Gospel of our Lord Jesus Christ. They will learn natural and civil things and holidays but nothing of spiritual value. The idea is that they have no proper knowledge of the nature of the gospel, and yet they see themselves as a superior acquaintance with its principles.

> *1 Corinthians 8:1-2 (ESV) Now concerning food offered to idols: we know that "all of us possess knowledge." This "knowledge" puffs up, but love builds up. 2 If anyone imagines that he knows something, he does not yet know as he ought to know.*

1 Timothy 6:4 (ESV) he is puffed up with conceit and understands nothing. <u>He has an unhealthy craving for controversy and for quarrels about words,</u> which produce envy, dissension, slander, evil suspicions,

Paul said these ungodly people love verbal disputes. This attitude indicates an ill-tempered and sickly condition, which turns away from the wholesome food of the gospel truth and the sweet character of our heavenly Father. It is a bad sign when society has become a people of unwholesome appetites, caring more for their fleshly appetites than for truth.

Paul isn't speaking about people who inquire or question in a genuine desire to learn. He mainly identifies those who ask questions or start discussions to show others they are the most intelligent people in the room or to create controversy. In one day, our Lord faced questions from the Pharisees, Sadducees, and a lawyer seeking to entrap Him.

> *Matthew 22:15-18 (ESV) Then the Pharisees went and plotted how to entangle him in his words. 16 And they sent their disciples to him, along with the Herodians, saying, "Teacher, we know that you are true and teach the way of God truthfully, and you do not care about anyone's opinion, for you are not swayed by appearances. 17 Tell us, then, what you think. Is it lawful to pay taxes to Caesar, or not?" 18 But Jesus, aware of their malice, said, "Why put me to the test, you hypocrites?*

> *Matthew 22:23-29 (ESV) The same day Sadducees came to him, who say that there is no resurrection, and they asked him a question, 24 saying, "Teacher, Moses said, 'If a man dies having no children, his brother must marry the widow and raise up offspring for his brother.' 25 Now there were seven brothers among us. The first married and died, and having no offspring left his wife to his brother. 26 So too the second and third, down to the seventh. 27 After them all, the woman died. 28 In the resurrection, therefore, of the seven, whose wife will she be? For they all had her." 29 But Jesus answered them, "You are wrong, because you know neither the Scriptures nor the power of God.*

> Matthew 22:34-36 (ESV) But when the Pharisees heard that he had silenced the Sadducees, they gathered together. 35 And one of them, a lawyer, asked him a question to test him. 36 "Teacher, which is the great commandment in the Law?"

Our Lord placed the religious leaders on the spot by asking them questions that would reveal their hearts. Instead of answering the questions, they remained silent and dared not test Him again with questions meant to entrap.

> Matthew 22:41-46 (ESV) Now while the Pharisees were gathered together, Jesus asked them a question, 42 saying, "What do you think about the Christ? Whose son is he?" They said to him, "The son of David." 43 He said to them, "How is it then that David, in the Spirit, calls him Lord, saying, 44 "'The Lord said to my Lord, "Sit at my right hand, until I put your enemies under your feet"'? 45 If then David calls him Lord, how is he his son?" 46 And no one was able to answer him a word, nor from that day did anyone dare to ask him any more questions.

The bottom line is this.

Come Out From Among Them

Chapter 22

Withdraw From Those That Teach Unsound Doctrine
1 Timothy 6:4-5
Part 6

1 Timothy 6:4-5 (ESV) he is puffed up with conceit and understands nothing. He has an unhealthy craving for controversy and for quarrels about words, which produce <u>envy, dissension, slander, evil suspicions</u>, 5 and constant friction among people who are depraved in mind and deprived of the truth, <u>imagining that godliness is a means of gain.</u>

The carnal and sensual appetite of those who are spiritually and morally sick was displayed by this list of unwholesome words in 1 Timothy 6:4-5.

No one believes that worldly gain is godliness or leads to godliness. The opposite is true, as stated by the apostle Paul in 1 Timothy 6:5. Many, down through the ages, have been guilty of using godliness to amass gain. In other words, these men, corrupted as they were in mind, in the whole inner life, and absent of the truth, only professed the Christian faith so far as it was serviceable to their worldly interests. Don't we need to hear these words today as a warning for what we see on our mass media from some so-called men of God?

Envy, strife, reviling, and evil suspicions are the fruit of the disputes and arguments of those who misuse God's truth. Those who operate in these sensual sins in the church body are the source of division and discontent. Though they may appear to be experts on the Bible, they damage the fellowship of God's corporate body of believers. Therefore, Paul warned Timothy, "From such, withdraw yourself." Paul was addressing young Timothy concerning his age and his position in the ministry. Paul was telling Timothy to expect such ungodly people to attack his ministry.

- *They would envy him and his office, wishing they had it.*
- *They would create strife among the fellowship of believers.*
- *They would promote friction against Timothy and other leaders in the church.*
- *They would be the source of evil suspicions against Timothy and other leaders in the church of evil motives and plots.*
- *Timothy and his church leaders needed this warning because such dangerous people in the church are not as apparent and easy to spot as one might think.*

1 Timothy 6:5 (ESV) and constant friction among people who are depraved in mind and deprived of the truth, <u>imagining that godliness is a means of gain.</u>

Paul told Timothy (and us) to watch for those who suppose that godliness is a means of personal gain. This false belief is another characteristic of those who misuse God's truth. Their interest in the things of God is not entirely for God's glory but motivated in part by their desire for wealth and comfort. These men believe the Christian faith is measured by the gain it brings. Paul forbids the servants of Christ from having any dealings with such men.

It is a sad commentary of our times, but Christianity is commonly presented today based on what you will gain by following Jesus instead of losing your life in Him. Today's message states if we follow Jesus, we will have personal success, happiness, a stronger family, and a more secure life. These things are true to some degree, but we must never market the Word of God and salvation as a product that will fix every life problem and bring personal gain.

When the gospel is marketed this way, it makes the followers of Jesus completely unprepared to handle the tough times. After all, if following the "Jesus" brand isn't working, why not try another brand?

This sales approach of *"what is in it for me"* gospel takes the focus off our Lord Jesus Christ and puts it on us and what He will give us. Many have their hearts only set on the blessings, not the One who blesses them.

While not ignoring the blessings of following Jesus Christ, we must not focus on them or allow them to be our motivation. We must proclaim the need to follow Jesus because He is God. We love Him because He first loved us, and we follow because of that love relationship. Yes, we owe Him everything as our Creator. We owe a debt we cannot pay, and He paid a debt He did not owe.

Doing what is right before God out of a love relationship and faith pleases and glorifies Him. Pleasing the

Come Out From Among Them

Father is far more important than whatever benefit and blessing we may have gained. Paul's warning to Timothy was to watch for believers who were more concerned with "What's in it for me" than their need to seek what glorifies the Father.

The bottom line is this.
Come Out From Among Them

Chapter 23

Withdraw From Those That Teach Unsound Doctrine
1 Timothy 6:5
Part 7

1 Timothy 6:5
From Such Withdraw Thyself.

The Apostle Paul warned young Timothy that envy, strife, reviling, and evil suspicions would come against him within the church. As we said before, this misbehavior and attack are the fruit of the disputes and arguments of those who misuse God's truth. Their presence in a church body is the source of division and discontent. They are very religious denominational, attend all the services, carry their Bibles, and may appear experts in God's Word. Paul admonished Timothy, "From such, withdraw yourself."

The term "From such withdraw yourself" is not in most manuscripts. It is added to the KJV Bible.

1 Timothy 6:5 (KJV) Perverse disputings of men of corrupt minds, and destitute of the truth, supposing that gain is godliness: <u>from such withdraw thyself.</u>

The Vulgate Latin and Ethiopic versions omit this clause. Even though the phrase "from such withdraw thyself" in 1 Timothy 6:5 seems to be added to the KJV and is missing in the older manuscripts, the teaching is consistent with other Scriptures and should be seen as the course of action to be taken.

The phrase "from such withdraw thyself" means that we do not come near them, have nothing to do with them, do not lay hands on them, admit them into the ministry, do not allow them to preach, or encourage them by hearing them. If they are in the church, we are to cast them out, not have communion with them in either a civil or religious way. We are to avoid all conversations with them.

Paul said in 1 Thessalonians 5:22 that we are to avoid or abstain from all appearance of evil. In Ephesians 5:11, Paul commands that we are to have no fellowship with the unfruitful works of darkness.

1 Thessalonians 5:22 (ESV) <u>Abstain</u> from every form of evil.

Ephesians 5:11 (ESV) <u>Take no part in</u> the unfruitful works of darkness, but instead <u>expose them</u>.

Of course, we have already covered Romans 15:16 with the command to avoid those who cause divisions. We talked about 2 Thessalonians 3:6 to keep away from Christians who walk in idleness.

Romans 16:17 (ESV) I appeal to you, brothers, to watch out for those who cause divisions and create obstacles contrary to the doctrine that you have been taught; <u>avoid them</u>.

2 Thessalonians 3:6 (ESV) Now we command you, brothers, in the name of our Lord Jesus Christ, that you <u>keep away from any brother who is walking in idleness</u> and not in accord with the tradition that you received from us.

In 2 Thessalonians 3:14, we are commanded to mark those believers who reject sound doctrine and have nothing to do with them.

2 Thessalonians 3:14-15 (ESV) If anyone does not obey what we say in this letter, <u>take note of that person, and have nothing to do with him,</u> that he may be ashamed. 15 Do not regard him as an enemy, but warn him as a brother.

In 1 Corinthians 5:9, Paul commanded us not to associate with those in the church who are sexually immoral. He told us in 5:13 to purge them from among us.

1 Corinthians 5:9 (ESV) I wrote to you in my letter <u>not to associate with</u> sexually immoral people—

1 Corinthians 5:13 (ESV) God judges those outside. "<u>Purge the evil person from among you.</u>"

Like us, Timothy needed this warning because such dangerous people are not as apparent as one might think. They are very religious and often the most active within the church. If you listen to their motive for church growth, you will hear them measure Christianity by the gain it brings. In response, Paul forbids Christian believers from having any dealings with such men.

Timothy told us not to associate with those who receive or present the gospel with this marketing approach.

Paul not only forbids Timothy from imitating these men but tells him to avoid them as harmful diseases. These men do not openly oppose the Gospel but make a profession of it, yet their company is infectious. Greed breeds greed. Paul understood the principle of "guilty by association."

1 Corinthians 15:33 (ESV) Do not be deceived: "Bad company ruins good morals."

There stood the danger that these greedy religious men would use genuine Christian love and acceptance of the church to incorporate themselves into the church's graces and favor. Remember, bad company ruins good morals.

The idea of "do not come near them" means Timothy and the church were to have nothing to do with those who continue to sin without repentance. They were not to lay hands on them for anointing or admit them into the ministry. They were not to allow them to speak the Word and spread their worldly doctrine.

We must not allow the emotion of love to cause us to disobey the Word of God. If we truly love the Father, His Word, and His people, we will be obedient and disfellowship those in our fellowship who refuse to confess and repent from their sins. We are to continue to love them. Exercising church discipline does not mean we are unloving. It does mean we love God and His Word over false fellowship and worldly, immoral behavior in the church.

Charles W Morris

The bottom line is this.
Come Out From Among Them

More Books By Charles Morris

1. *15 Ways To Hear The Voice Of God (2019 06 25 Unpublished)*
2. *A Course In Miracles (2023 07 24)*
3. *A Willingness To Be Taught (2021 12 03)*
4. *Angels (2023 07 31)*
5. *Be Healed (2024 03 02)*
6. *Born Again (2021 07 09)*
7. *Chart Your Path Bible Study Journal (2020 11 18)*
8. *Devotional Bible Series Volume 1 Defeating The Sin Within Me (2023 11 24)*
9. *Devotional Bible Series Volume 2 A Backsliding Heart (2023 11 26)*
10. *Devotional Bible Series Volume 3 Six Enemies Of Faith (2023 01 17)*
11. *Devotional Bible Series Volume 4 The Spiritual Man (2023 11 28)*
12. *Devotional Bible Series Volume 5 Intimate Deception- What Are The Six Dangerous Love Affairs (2023 01 19)*
13. *Devotional Bible Series Volume 6 Setting The Heart (2023 12 14)*
14. *Devotional Bible Series Volume 7 Dare To Pray (2023 12 15)*
15. *Devotional Bible Series Volume 8 Be A Voice, Not An Echo (2024 08 02)*
16. *Don't Give The Enemy A Seat At Your Table (2023 07 02)*
17. *Experiencing The Beauty Of Brokenness (2020 02 07)*
18. *Faithful (2019 12 29 Unpublished)*
19. *Fifteen Ways To Hear The Voice Of God (2021 06 09 Unpublished)*
20. *Gifts From God*

21. *Go Tell It On The Mountain (2022 11 16)*
22. *God Is Online German (2012 02 09)*
23. *He Speaks Volume 1: He Speaks To Us Through The Holy Spirit*
24. *He Speaks Volume 2: He Speaks To Us Through The Bible.*
25. *He Speaks Volume 3: He Speaks To Us Through Prayer And Fasting.*
26. *Hosea (2021 05 27)*
27. *Hosea 1 Introduction (2021 10 02)*
28. *Hosea 1_1-3 (2021 10 02)*
29. *Hosea 1_4-5 (2021 10 03)*
30. *Hosea 1_6-7 (2021 10 03)*
31. *Hosea 1_8-9 (2021 10 03)*
32. *Hosea 1_10-11 The Ultimate Promise (2021 12 03 Unpublished)*
33. *Host The Holy Ghost (2023 10 29)*
34. *How Do I Write A Book (2020 02 05)*
35. *I Am Statements Journals Light Blue (2023 01 17)*
36. *I Am Statements Journals Dark Blue (2023 01 17)*
37. *I Am Statements Journals Gold (2023 01 17)*
38. *I Am Statements Journals Light Pink (2023 01 17)*
39. *I Am Statements Journals Dark Pink (2023 01 17)*
40. *I Am Statements Journals Peach (2023 01 17)*
41. *I Feel Like I'm Losing My Faith (2022 06 28)*
42. *Is Atheism Dead (2022 02 20)*
43. *Is Christian Immaturity Dead (2022 09 02)*
44. *Is Religion Dead The Believing Unbeliever (2022 06 18)*
45. *Just Give Me One More (2024 01 27)*
46. *Luke 15 (2021 12 07 Unpublished)*
47. *My Topical Journal (2020 11 04 Unpublished)*
48. *Our Holy Treasure (2024 01 29)*
49. *Overcoming Fear (2023 05 27)*
50. *Places Where God And Man Meet (2021 09 25)*
51. *Prayer And His Presence (2024 07 11)*

52. *Preparing Ourselves To Hear God's Voice (2019 06 24 Unpublished)*
53. *Preparing Ourselves To Hear The Voice Of God (2021 06 09)*
54. *The 10 Characteristics Of A Spirit Filled Church (2020 03 22)*
55. *The 24 Qualifications Of An Elder (2021 07 02)*
56. *The Bible Proves Itself True (2021 09 02)*
57. *The Chronological Book Of End Times (2022 03 16)*
58. *The Cost Of Discipleship (2022 11 23)*
59. *The Covenant Of Salt (2021 10 03)*
60. *The Five Evidences Of Salvation (2021 09 09)*
61. *The Five Witnesses Of Salvation (2019 06 06)*
62. *The Four Positions Of The Holy Spirit (2014 02 18)*
63. *The Four Positions Of The Holy Spirit (2021 10 02)*
64. *The Gifts Of The Holy Spirit (2024 03 27)*
65. *The Gospel According To Jesus (2023 01 14)*
66. *The Gospel According To Luke_Luke 15 (2022 12 19)*
67. *The Holy Bible-The King James Version Of The Old And New Testaments Annotated (2022 08 06 Unpublished)*
68. *The Holy Spirit-Do I Have To Speak In Tongues (2023 08 07)*
69. *The Mystery Of Lawlessness Unleased (2021 12 21 Unpublished)*
70. *The Parable Of The Four Soils (2021 06 22)*
71. *The Parable Of The Wheat And Tares (2022 10 08) The Power Of One More (2022 12 02 Unpublished)*
72. *The Topical Journal Don't Just Sit There, Journal For Businessmen (2022 03 16)*
73. *The Topical Journal Don't Just Sit There, Journal Purple (2022 03 15)*
74. *The Topical Journal, Journal Like A Veteran (2022 03 12)*
75. *The Topical Journal, Journaling That Impacts Your Life Pink (2022 03 15)*

76. *Unleashed: Understanding The Mystery Of Lawlessness (2022 06 25)*
77. *We Need Faith (2022 07 24)*
78. *Wherever You Go Travel Journal Beach Buggy (2022 03 03)*
79. *Wherever You Go Travel Journal Hiking For Teens (2022 03 07)*
80. *Wherever You Go Travel Journal Jeep For The Guys (2022 03 04)*
81. *Whisper: Discerning The Not God Voices (2024 02 12)*
82. *Your Dash (2020 11 17)*

About The Author

CHARLES MORRIS has a rich legacy spanning 49 years as a dedicated servant of God to the body of Christ. His diverse roles as a pastor, church planter, evangelist, house church coordinator, and prolific author of over 70 books have left a profound impact on countless lives.

As the visionary founder and CEO of RSI Ministry and Raising the Standard International Publishing, Pastor Charles remains committed to inspiring believers to walk in God's holiness through the power and presence of the Holy Spirit.

Passionate about living according to God's standards, he tirelessly calls the church to embody Christ's likeness in their daily lives in word, deed and thought. Pastor Charles firmly believes in the significance of genuine salvation, encouraging all believers to examine their lives through the lens of God's Word.

Currently residing in Navarre, Florida, Pastor Charles finds unwavering support and partnership in life with his beloved wife, Debra.

Made in the USA
Monee, IL
18 March 2025

14213311R00075